Everyday Mathematics®

Home Links

Everyday Mathematics®

Home Links

**The University of Chicago
School Mathematics Project**

A Division of The McGraw·Hill Companies

Columbus, Ohio
Chicago, Illinois

UCSMP Elementary Materials Component

Max Bell, Director

Authors

Max Bell
Jean Bell
John Bretzlauf*
Amy Dillard*
Robert Hartfield

Andy Isaacs*
James McBride, Director
Kathleen Pitvorec*
Peter Saecker

Technical Art

Diana Barrie*

Second Edition only

Contributors

Librada Acosta, Carol Arkin, Robert Balfanz, Sharlean Brooks,
Jean Callahan, Anne Coglianese, Ellen Dairyko, Tresea Felder,
James Flanders, Dorothy Freedman, Rita Gronbach, Deborah Arron Leslie,
William D. Pattison, LaDonna Pitts, Danette Riehle, Marie Schilling,
Robert Strang, Sadako Tengan, There Wasik, Leeann Wille, Michael Wilson

Photo Credits

Phil Martin/Photography, Jack Demuth/Photography, Cover Credits: Bee/Stephen Dalton/Photo
Researchers Inc., Photo Collage: Herman Adler Design

Permissions

page 103: Cylindars/cans: Jack Demuth
page 103: Quilt: Gary Conner/PhotoEdit
page 103: Robert Brenner, Empire State Builing/PhotoEdit
page 156: John Lee/*Chicago Tribune*

www.sra4kids.com

SRA/McGraw-Hill

A Division of The McGraw·Hill Companies

Send all inquiries to:
SRA/McGraw-Hill
P.O. Box 812960
Chicago, IL 60681

Printed in the United States of America.

ISBN 1-57039-945-x

9 10 11 12 VL 07 06 05 04

Contents

Family Letter

Introduction to Second Grade Everyday Mathematics

Welcome to *Second Grade Everyday Mathematics*. It is a part of an elementary school mathematics curriculum developed by the University of Chicago School Mathematics Project.

Several features of the program are described below to help familiarize you with the structure and expectations of *Everyday Mathematics*.

A problem-solving approach based on everyday situations By making connections between their own knowledge and their experiences both in school and outside of school, children learn basic math skills in meaningful contexts so that the mathematics becomes "real."

Frequent practice of basic skills Instead of practice presented in a single, tedious drill format, children practice basic skills in a variety of more engaging ways. In addition to completing daily review exercises covering a variety of topics, patterning on the number grid, and working with addition and subtraction fact families in different formats, children will play games that are specifically designed to develop basic skills.

An instructional approach that revisits concepts regularly To enhance the development of basic skills and concepts, children regularly revisit previously learned concepts and repeatedly practice skills encountered earlier. The lessons are designed to take advantage of previously learned concepts and skills and to build on them throughout the year instead of treating them as isolated bits of knowledge.

A curriculum that explores mathematical content beyond basic arithmetic Mathematics standards around the world indicate that basic arithmetic skills are only the beginning of the mathematical knowledge children will need as they develop critical-thinking skills. In addition to basic arithmetic, *Everyday Mathematics* develops concepts and skills in the following topics—numeration; operations and computation; data and chance; geometry; measurement and reference frames; and patterns, functions, and algebra.

Second Grade Everyday Mathematics emphasizes the following content:

Numeration Counting; reading and writing numbers; identifying place value; comparing numbers; working with fractions; using money to develop place value and decimal concepts

Operations and Computation Recalling addition and subtraction facts; exploring fact families (related addition and subtraction facts, such as $2 + 5 = 7$, $5 + 2 = 7$, $7 - 5 = 2$, and $7 - 2 = 5$); adding and subtracting with tens and hundreds; beginning multiplication and division; exchanging money amounts

Data and Chance Collecting, organizing, and interpreting data using tables, charts, and graphs

Geometry Exploring 2- and 3-dimensional shapes; classifying polygons

Measurement Using tools to measure length, weight, capacity, and volume; using U.S. customary and metric measurement units, such as feet, centimeters, ounces, and grams

Reference Frames Using clocks, calendars, thermometers, and number lines

Patterns, Functions, and Algebra Exploring number patterns, rules for number sequences, relations between numbers, and attributes

Everyday Mathematics provides you with ample opportunities to monitor your child's progress and to participate in your child's mathematics experiences.

Throughout the year, you will receive Family Letters to keep you informed of the mathematical content that your child will be studying in each unit. Each letter includes a vocabulary list, suggested Do-Anytime Activities for you and your child, and an answer guide to selected Home Link (homework) activities.

You will enjoy seeing your child's confidence and comprehension soar as he or she connects mathematics to everyday life.

We look forward to an exciting year!

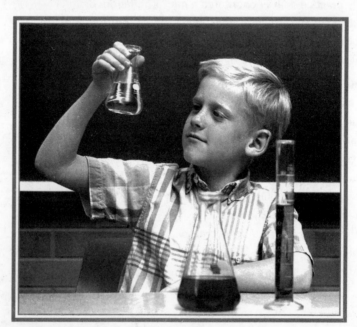

Relations: $<$, $>$, $=$

Family Note

In *Second Grade Everyday Mathematics,* children "do mathematics." We expect that children will want to share their enthusiasm for the mathematics activities they do in school with their families. Your child will bring home assignments and activities to do as homework throughout the year. These assignments, called "Home Links," will be identified by the house at the top right corner of this page. The assignments will not take very much time to complete, but most of them involve interaction with an adult or an older child.

There are many reasons for including Home Links in the second grade program:

· The assignments encourage children to take initiative and responsibility for completing them. As you respond with encouragement and assistance, you help your child build independence and self-confidence.

· Home Links reinforce newly learned skills and concepts. They provide opportunities for children to think and practice at their own pace.

· These assignments are often designed to relate what is done in school to children's lives outside school. This helps tie mathematics to the real world, which is very important in the *Everyday Mathematics* program.

· The Home Links assignments will help you get a better idea of the mathematics your child is learning in school.

Generally, you can help by listening and responding to your child's requests and comments about mathematics. You also can help by linking numbers to real life, pointing out ways in which you use numbers (time, TV channels, page numbers, telephone numbers, bus routes, shopping lists, and so on). Extending the notion that "children who are read to, read," *Everyday Mathematics* supports the belief that children who have someone do math with them will learn mathematics. Playful counting and thinking games that are fun for both you and your child are very helpful for such learning.

*Please return the **second page** of this Home Link to school tomorrow.*

Temperatures

Family Note

In today's lesson, the class examined thermometers and practiced reading Fahrenheit temperatures. We began a daily routine of recording the outside temperature. If you have a nondigital thermometer at home (inside or outside), encourage your child to read the Fahrenheit temperatures to you. We will introduce Celsius temperatures in a later unit.

Please return this Home Link to school tomorrow.

1. Circle the thermometer that shows 30°F.

2. Circle the thermometer that shows 20°F.

3. Circle the thermometer that shows 12°F.

4. Circle the thermometer that shows 28°F.

Family Letter

Unit 2: Addition and Subtraction Facts

Unit 2 focuses on reviewing and extending addition facts and linking subtraction to addition. Children will solve basic addition and subtraction facts through real-life stories.

In *Everyday Mathematics*, the ability to recall number facts instantly is called "fact power." Instant recall of the addition and subtraction facts will become a powerful tool in computation with multidigit numbers, such as 29 + 92.

Math Tools

Your child will be using **Fact Triangles** to practice and review addition and subtraction facts. Fact Triangles are a "new and improved" version of flash cards; the addition and subtraction facts shown are made from the same three numbers, helping your child understand the relationships among those facts. The Family Note on Home Link 2.8, which you will receive later, provides a more detailed description of Fact Triangles.

The dot designates the largest number.

A Fact Triangle showing the fact family for 3, 8, and 11

Vocabulary

Important terms in Unit 2:

label A unit, descriptive word, or phrase used to put a number or numbers in context. Using a label reinforces the idea that numbers always refer to something.

unit box A box that contains the label or unit of measure for the numbers in a problem. For example, in number stories involving children in the class, the unit box would be as follows:

A unit box allows children to remember that numbers have a context without having to repeat the label in each problem.

number story A story made up by children, teachers, or parents. It contains a problem that can be solved by using one or more of the four basic operations.

number model A number sentence that shows how the parts of a number story are related. For example, 5 + 8 = 13 shows how the parts are related in this number story: "5 children skating. 8 children playing ball. How many children in all?"

fact power The ability to instantly recall basic number facts.

doubles fact The sum or product of the same two 1-digit numbers, such as 2 + 2 = 4 or 3 × 3 = 9.

turn-around facts A pair of addition (or multiplication) facts in which the order of the addends (or factors) is reversed, such as 3 + 5 = 8 and 5 + 3 = 8 (or 3 × 4 = 12 and 4 × 3 = 12). If you know an addition or multiplication fact, you also know its turnaround.

fact family A collection of addition and subtraction facts (and later, multiplication and division facts) made from the same three numbers. For example, the addition/subtraction fact family for the numbers 2, 4, and 6 consists of $2 + 4 = 6$, $4 + 2 = 6$, $6 - 4 = 2$, and $6 - 2 = 4$. The multiplication/division fact family for the numbers 2, 4, and 8 consists of $2 \times 4 = 8$, $4 \times 2 = 8$, $8 \div 2 = 4$, and $8 \div 4 = 2$.

Frames-and-Arrows diagram A diagram used to represent a number sequence, or a set of numbers that are ordered according to a rule. A Frames-and-Arrows diagram consists of frames connected by arrows to show the path from one frame to the next. Each frame contains a number in the sequence; each arrow represents a rule that determines which number goes in the next frame.

"What's My Rule?" table A list of number pairs in which the numbers in each pair are related according to the same rule. This relationship can be represented by a **function machine,** an imaginary device that processes numbers according to the rule. A number (input) is put into the machine and is transformed into a second number (output) through the application of the rule.

Function machine

in	out
3	8
5	10
8	13

"What's My Rule?"
table

Do-Anytime Activities

To work with your child on the concepts taught in this unit and in previous units, try these interesting and rewarding activities:

1 Talk with your child about why it is important to learn basic facts.

2 Create addition and subtraction stories about given subjects.

3 Have your child explain how to use a facts table.

4 As you discover which facts your child is having difficulty mastering, make a Fact Triangle using the three numbers of that fact family.

5 Name a number and ask your child to think of several different ways to represent that number. For example, 10 can be represented as $9 + 1$, $5 + 5$, $14 - 4$, and so on.

10	
ten	$12 - 2$
$1 + 9$	$6 + 4$
diez	$10 - 0$

Use with Lesson 1.14.

Addition Facts Maze

Family Note

For homework, your child will review addition facts like the ones we have been working on in class. To help identify the path from the child to the ice cream cone, have your child circle the sums of 9, 10, and 11.

Please return this Home Link to school tomorrow.

Help the child find the ice cream. Answer all the problems. Then draw the child's path by connecting facts with sums of 9, 10, or 11. You can move up, down, left, or right as you move between boxes.

	$\begin{array}{r}2\\+6\\\hline\end{array}$ 8	$\begin{array}{r}2\\+5\\\hline\end{array}$ 7	$\begin{array}{r}1\\+6\\\hline\end{array}$ 7	$\begin{array}{r}0\\+8\\\hline\end{array}$ 8	$\begin{array}{r}5\\+7\\\hline\end{array}$ 13	$\begin{array}{r}3\\+9\\\hline\end{array}$ 12	$\begin{array}{r}7\\+0\\\hline\end{array}$ 7	$\begin{array}{r}4\\+4\\\hline\end{array}$ 8	$\begin{array}{r}1\\+5\\\hline\end{array}$ 6	$\begin{array}{r}4\\+3\\\hline\end{array}$ 7
$\begin{array}{r}2\\+7\\\hline\end{array}$ 9	$\begin{array}{r}6\\+5\\\hline\end{array}$ 11	$\begin{array}{r}1\\+7\\\hline\end{array}$ 8	$\begin{array}{r}3\\+5\\\hline\end{array}$ 8	$\begin{array}{r}6\\+3\\\hline\end{array}$ 9	$\begin{array}{r}1\\+8\\\hline\end{array}$ 9	$\begin{array}{r}8\\+2\\\hline\end{array}$ 10	$\begin{array}{r}5\\+3\\\hline\end{array}$ 8	$\begin{array}{r}2\\+4\\\hline\end{array}$ 6	$\begin{array}{r}3\\+3\\\hline\end{array}$ 6	$\begin{array}{r}8\\+7\\\hline\end{array}$ 15
$\begin{array}{r}4\\+4\\\hline\end{array}$ 8	$\begin{array}{r}5\\+4\\\hline\end{array}$ 9	$\begin{array}{r}9\\+3\\\hline\end{array}$ 12	$\begin{array}{r}0\\+9\\\hline\end{array}$ 9	$\begin{array}{r}4\\+6\\\hline\end{array}$ 10	$\begin{array}{r}7\\+1\\\hline\end{array}$ 8	$\begin{array}{r}5\\+5\\\hline\end{array}$ 10	$\begin{array}{r}8\\+0\\\hline\end{array}$ 8	$\begin{array}{r}5\\+9\\\hline\end{array}$ 14	$\begin{array}{r}6\\+7\\\hline\end{array}$ 14	$\begin{array}{r}6\\+1\\\hline\end{array}$ 7
$\begin{array}{r}6\\+2\\\hline\end{array}$ 8	$\begin{array}{r}3\\+8\\\hline\end{array}$ 11	$\begin{array}{r}7\\+4\\\hline\end{array}$ 11	$\begin{array}{r}9\\+2\\\hline\end{array}$ 12	$\begin{array}{r}5\\+3\\\hline\end{array}$	$\begin{array}{r}4\\+4\\\hline\end{array}$	$\begin{array}{r}2\\+9\\\hline\end{array}$	$\begin{array}{r}4\\+8\\\hline\end{array}$	$\begin{array}{r}4\\+9\\\hline\end{array}$	$\begin{array}{r}1\\+1\\\hline\end{array}$ 2	$\begin{array}{r}5\\+2\\\hline\end{array}$ 7
$\begin{array}{r}3\\+4\\\hline\end{array}$	$\begin{array}{r}6\\+6\\\hline\end{array}$	$\begin{array}{r}8\\+4\\\hline\end{array}$	$\begin{array}{r}7\\+5\\\hline\end{array}$	$\begin{array}{r}7\\+0\\\hline\end{array}$ 7	$\begin{array}{r}6\\+2\\\hline\end{array}$	$\begin{array}{r}7\\+3\\\hline\end{array}$	$\begin{array}{r}3\\+6\\\hline\end{array}$	$\begin{array}{r}4\\+7\\\hline\end{array}$	$\begin{array}{r}6\\+8\\\hline\end{array}$	$\begin{array}{r}5\\+6\\\hline\end{array}$
$\begin{array}{r}8\\+5\\\hline\end{array}$	$\begin{array}{r}3\\+6\\\hline\end{array}$	$\begin{array}{r}4\\+7\\\hline\end{array}$	$\begin{array}{r}5\\+2\\\hline\end{array}$	$\begin{array}{r}1\\+6\\\hline\end{array}$	$\begin{array}{r}3\\+5\\\hline\end{array}$	$\begin{array}{r}6\\+7\\\hline\end{array}$	$\begin{array}{r}5\\+7\\\hline\end{array}$	$\begin{array}{r}8\\+3\\\hline\end{array}$	$\begin{array}{r}7\\+7\\\hline\end{array}$	$\begin{array}{r}9\\+4\\\hline\end{array}$
$\begin{array}{r}6\\+1\\\hline\end{array}$ 7	$\begin{array}{r}8\\+4\\\hline\end{array}$	$\begin{array}{r}2\\+6\\\hline\end{array}$ 14	$\begin{array}{r}7\\+7\\\hline\end{array}$ 1	$\begin{array}{r}4\\+2\\\hline\end{array}$ 5	$\begin{array}{r}1\\+4\\\hline\end{array}$	$\begin{array}{r}0\\+7\\\hline\end{array}$	$\begin{array}{r}3\\+9\\\hline\end{array}$	$\begin{array}{r}4\\+5\\\hline\end{array}$	$\begin{array}{r}6\\+4\\\hline\end{array}$	

Weighing Things

Family Note

Today we worked with a pan balance to compare the weights of objects. We used a spring scale to weigh objects up to a pound. We introduced the word *ounce* as a unit of weight for light objects.

*Please return the **second page** of this Home Link to school tomorrow.*

1. Tell someone at home about how you used the pan balance to compare the weights of two objects.

2. Tell someone at home how you used the spring scale to weigh objects.

Fact Triangles

**Family
Note**

Fact Triangles are tools used to help build mental arithmetic skills. You might think of them as the *Everyday Mathematics* version of flash cards. Fact Triangles are more effective for helping children memorize facts, however, because of their emphasis on fact families. A **fact family** is a collection of related addition and subtraction facts that use the same 3 numbers. The fact family for the numbers 2, 4, and 6 consists of 2 + 4 = 6, 4 + 2 = 6, 6 − 4 = 2, and 6 − 2 = 4.

   To use Fact Triangles to practice addition with your child, cover the number next to the large dot with your thumb.

   Your child tells you the addition fact: 4 + 5 = 9 or 5 + 4 = 9.

   To use Fact Triangles to practice subtraction, cover one of the numbers in the lower corners with your thumb.

   Your child tells you the subtraction facts: 9 − 5 = 4 and 9 − 4 = 5.

   If your child misses a fact, flash the other two fact problems on the card and then return to the fact that was missed.

   Example: Sue can't answer 9 − 5. Flash 4 + 5, then 9 − 4, and finally 9 − 5 a second time.

   Make this activity brief and fun. Spend about 10 minutes each night over the next few weeks or until your child masters all of the facts. The work that you do at home will help your child develop an instant recall of facts and will complement the work that we are doing at school.

Frames-and-Arrows Problems

Family Note

Today your child used **Frames-and-Arrows diagrams.** These diagrams show sequences of numbers—numbers that follow one after the other according to a rule. Frames-and-Arrows diagrams are made up of shapes called *frames* and arrows that connect the frames. Each frame contains one of the numbers in the sequence. Each *arrow* stands for a rule that tells which number goes in the next frame. Here is an example of a Frames-and-Arrows diagram. The arrow rule is "Add 2."

Rule
Add 2

2   4   6   8   10

In a Frames-and-Arrows problem, some of the information is left out. To solve the problem, you have to find the missing information. Here are two examples of Frames-and-Arrows problems:

Example 1: Fill in the empty frames according to the rule.

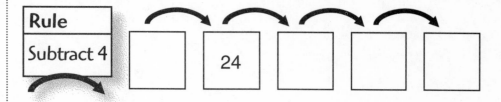

Rule
Subtract 4

☐   24   ☐   ☐   ☐

Solution: Write 28, 20, 16, and 12 in the empty frames.

Example 2: Write the arrow rule in the empty box.

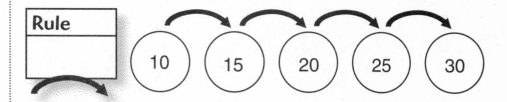

Rule

10   15   20   25   30

Solution: The arrow rule is Add 5, or +5.

Ask your child to tell you about Frames-and-Arrows diagrams. Take turns making u̶ and solving Frames-and-Arrows problems like the examples above with your child.

*Please return the **second page** of this Home Link to school tomorrow.*

"What's My Rule?"

Family Note

Today your child learned about a kind of problem you may not have seen before. We call it "What's My Rule?" Please ask your child to explain it to you.

    Here is a little background information: Imagine a machine with a funnel at the top and a tube coming out of the bottom. The machine can be programmed so that if a number is dropped into the funnel, the machine does something to the number, and a new number comes out the tube. For example, the machine could be programmed to add 5 to any number that is dropped in. If you put in 3, out would come 8. If you put in 7, out would come 12.

We call this device a *function machine*.

```
    3
    ↓
   in
  ┌──────┐
  │ Rule │
  ├──────┤
  │ +5   │
  └──────┘
    ↓
   out
    8
```

You can show the results of the rule "+5" in a table:

in	out
3	8
7	12
15	20

    In a "What's My Rule?" problem, some of the information is missing. To solve the problem, you have to find the missing information. The missing information could be the numbers that come out of a function machine, the numbers that are dropped in, or the rule for programming the machine. *For example:*

Rule
Add 6

in	out
3	
5	
8	

Missing:
"out" numbers

Rule

in	out
6	3
10	5
16	8

Missing:
rule

Rule
+4

in	out
	6
	16
	11

Missing:
"in" numbers

Like Frames-and-Arrows problems, "What's My Rule?" problems help children practice facts (and extended facts) in a problem-solving format.

*Please return the **second page** of this Home Link to school tomorrow.*

"What's My Rule?" (cont.)

Give the Family Note to someone at home. Show that person
how you can complete "What's My Rule?" tables. Show that
person how you can find rules.

1. Fill in the table.

Rule +9	
in	**out**
1	10
4	13
6	
8	
5	

2. Find the rule.

Rule	
in	**out**
10	2
12	4
9	1
14	6
8	0

3. Fill in the table.

Rule +6	
in	**out**
4	10
	12
	9
	15
	6

4. Challenge Find the rule. Fill in the table.

Rule	
in	**out**
8	13
4	9
13	
	10

5. Al read 5 more pages than Cindy.

If Cindy read 13 pages, how many pages did Al read?

_____ pages

If Al read 10 pages, how many pages did Cindy read?

_____ pages

Subtraction Maze

Family Note

For homework, your child will practice subtraction facts like the ones we have been working on in class. To help identify the path from the dog to the ball, have your child circle the differences of 3, 4, and 5.

Please return this Home Link to school tomorrow.

Help the dog find her ball. Solve all of the problems. Then draw the dog's path by connecting facts with answers of 3, 4, or 5. You can move up, down, left, right, or diagonally as you move between boxes.

8−4	12−6	8−8	4−0	5−4	9−7	10−3	5−2	6−0	18−9
8−7	16−8	6−1	7−3	4−2	12−3	5−1	9−8	8−6	6−3	7−6
5−1	3−3	9−2	11−0	7−2	3−2	12−6	8−3	3−1	8−0	6−4
10−2	5−0	7−1	9−3	11−2	10−5	12−1	7−0	4−3	14−7	3−0
5−3	12−0	2−1	8−1	6−5	12−2	6−2	2−2	7−5	10−9	9−0
11−3	4−1	9−1	2−0	10−1	9−9	8−5	3−0	11−1	10−7	11−8
10−0	5−5	10−9	8−2	10−8	11−9	6−6	12−3	9−6	7−4	

Use with Lesson 2.12.

Addition/Subtraction Facts (cont.)   Home Link 2.13

Cut out the Fact Triangles. Show someone at home how you use them to practice adding and subtracting.

Family Letter

Unit 3: Place Value, Money, and Time

In Unit 3, children will read, write, and compare numbers from 0 through 999, working on concepts and skills built upon since *Kindergarten Everyday Mathematics.* Your child will review *place value,* or the meaning of each digit in a number. For example, in the number 52, the 5 represents 5 tens, and the 2 represents 2 ones.

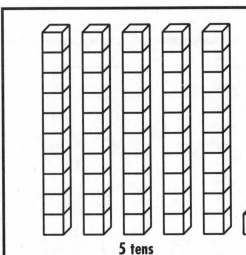

5 tens   2 ones

Your child will use base-10 blocks like these to help him or her understand the idea of place value.

Your child will also review money concepts, including finding the values of coins, identifying different coin combinations for the same amount, and making change.

43¢

43¢

43¢

Your child will read and record time using the hour and minute hands on an analog clock.

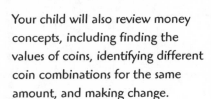

Vocabulary

Important terms in Unit 3:

analog clock A clock that shows time by the position of the hour and minute hands.

analog clock

digital clock A clock that shows time by using digits.

digital clock

data A collection of information, usually in the form of numbers. For example, the following data show the ages (in years) of six second graders: 6, 7, 6, 6, 7, 6.

middle number The number in the middle of a set of data when the data are organized in sequential order. For example, the numbers in this set of data are arranged from least to greatest:

2   3   (5)   8   10

The number 5 is the middle number of this set. The middle number is also called the *median*.

two-rule Frames and Arrows A diagram that shows a sequence of numbers, or numbers that follow one after the other according to two rules. For example, see the Frames-and-Arrows diagram below.

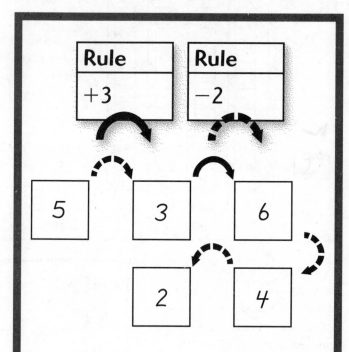

To go from the first square to the second square, use the rule for the dashed arrow.

$$5 - \mathbf{2} = 3$$

To go from the second square to the third square, use the rule for the solid arrow.

$$3 + \mathbf{3} = 6$$

Use with Lesson 2.14.

Do-Anytime Activities

To work with your child on the concepts taught in this unit and in previous units, try these interesting and rewarding activities:

1 Have your child tell the time shown on an analog clock.

2 Draw an analog clock face without hands. Say a time and have your child show it on the clock face.

3 At the grocery store, give your child an item that costs less than $1.00. Allow your child to pay for the item separately. Ask him or her to determine how much change is due and to check that the change received is correct.

4 Gather a handful of coins with a value less than $2.00. Have your child calculate the total value.

5 Reinforce place value in 2- and 3-digit numbers. For example, in the number 694, the digit 6 means 6 hundreds, or 600; the digit 9 means 9 tens, or 90; and the digit 4 means 4 ones, or 4.

As You Help Your Child with Homework

As your child brings home assignments, you may want to go over the instructions together, clarifying them as necessary. The answers listed below will guide you through this unit's Home Links.

Home Link 3.1

1. a. 374   **b.** 507   **2.** 740

3. 936   **4.** 8; 0; 6   **5.** 2; 3; 1

Home Link 3.3

2. 6:30   **3.** 2:15   **4.** 9:00   **5.** 1:30

6.

7.

8.

9.

Home Link 3.4

1. | Rule | *Sample answers:*
| Add 12 |

In	Out	Out in a different way
I	II ..	I :: ....
II	III	II ::::: :....
II	III	II ::::: :::..

2. | Rule |
| Add 16 |

In	Out	Out in a different way
IIII .	IIIII	IIII ::::: ::....
......	I :......	II .

Home Link 3.6

1. 40¢; 50¢; 55¢   **2.** 50¢; 45¢; 55¢

Home Link 3.8

5¢; 35¢; 16¢; 5¢; 2¢; 52¢

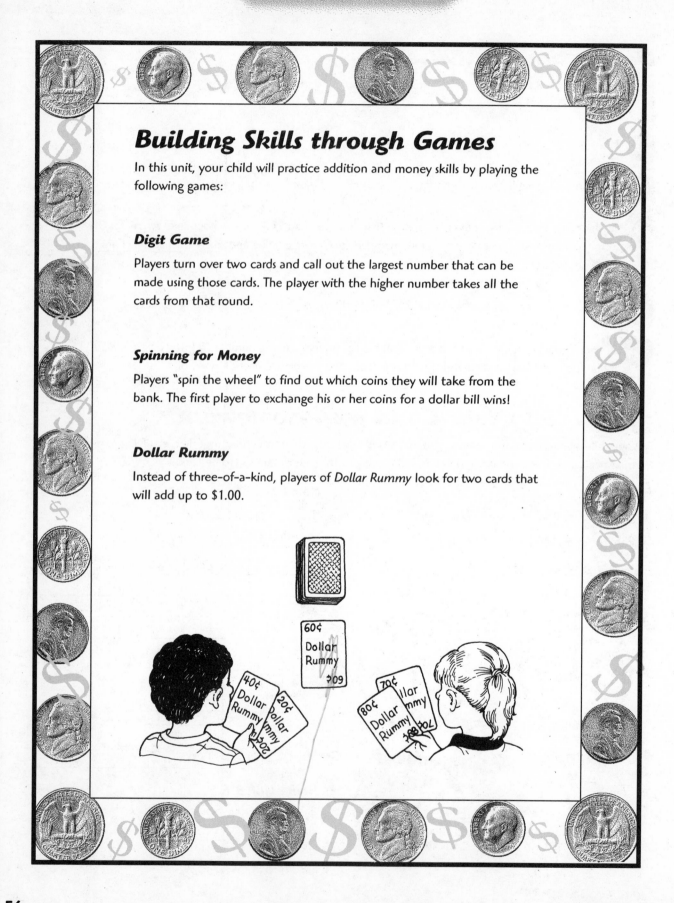

Building Skills through Games

In this unit, your child will practice addition and money skills by playing the following games:

Digit Game

Players turn over two cards and call out the largest number that can be made using those cards. The player with the higher number takes all the cards from that round.

Spinning for Money

Players "spin the wheel" to find out which coins they will take from the bank. The first player to exchange his or her coins for a dollar bill wins!

Dollar Rummy

Instead of three-of-a-kind, players of *Dollar Rummy* look for two cards that will add up to $1.00.

Use with Lesson 2.14.

Place Value

Family Note

All numbers are made up of digits. The value of a digit depends on its place in the number. In the number 704, the digit 7 means 7 hundreds, the digit 0 means 0 tens, and the digit 4 means 4 ones. This idea is called **place value.**

Your child has been using base-10 blocks to help him or her understand the idea of place value. Base-10 blocks are shown in Problems 1a and 1b below. A "cube" (with each side 1 unit long) represents 1. A "long" (a rod that is 10 units long) represents 10. And a "flat" (a square with each side 10 units long) represents 100.

Please return this Home Link to school tomorrow.

1. Which number do the base-10 blocks show?

a.

_800_

b.

_407_

2. Write a number with
7 in the hundreds place,
0 in the ones place, and
4 in the tens place.

_704_

3. Write a number with
3 in the tens place,
6 in the ones place, and
9 in the hundreds place.

_369_

4. In 806, how
many hundreds? _8_

How many tens? _0_

How many ones? _6_

5. In 231, how
many hundreds? _2_

How many tens? _3_

How many ones? _1_

How Much Does It Cost?

Family Note

In this activity, your child looks through advertisements, selects items that cost less than $2.00, and shows how to pay for those items in more than one way. For example, your child could pay for an item that costs 79¢ by drawing 3 quarters and 4 pennies or by drawing 7 dimes and 9 pennies. If you do not have advertisements showing prices, make up some items and prices for your child.

Please return this Home Link to school tomorrow.

Look at newspaper or magazine advertisements. Find items that cost less than $2.00. Write the name and price of each item.

Show someone at home how you would pay for these items with coins and a $1 bill. Write Ⓟ, Ⓝ, Ⓓ, Ⓠ, and $1 . Try to show amounts in more than one way.

1. I would buy _a pencil_. It costs _$100_.

This is one way I would pay: _____

This is another way: _make a dollar 2 QQQQQPP_

2. I would buy _a cat_. It costs _4 00 $_.

This is one way I would pay: _4   QQQQ_

This is another way: _____

3. I would buy _____. It costs _____.

This is one way I would pay: _____

This is another way: _____

Times of Day

Family Note

Your child has been learning how to tell time by writing times shown on an analog clock (a clock with an hour hand and a minute hand) and by setting the hands on an analog clock to show a specific time. To complete the exercises on this page, your child will need a paper clock or a real clock with an hour hand and a minute hand. You can make a clock from *Math Masters,* page 40. Ask your child to show you other times on his or her clock.

Please return this Home Link to school tomorrow.

1. Use your clock to show someone at home the time you do the following activities. Write the time under each activity.

Eat dinner	Go to bed	Get up	Eat lunch
7 : 00	80 : 00	6 : 00	2 : 00

Write the time.

2.

6 : 40

3.

2 : 20

Times of Day (cont.)

4.

9 : 00

5.

6 : 30

Draw the hands to match the time.

6.

4:00

7.

9:30

8.

12:45

9.

10:15

"What's My Rule?" with Blocks

Family Note

Your child will complete the tables on this page by drawing tens and ones for 2-digit numbers. More than one picture can be drawn for a number. For example, to show 26, your child might draw 2 tens and 6 ones, 1 ten and 16 ones, or 26 ones. The symbol | stands for 10, and the symbol ▪ stands for 1.

Please return this Home Link to school tomorrow.

1. Draw simple pictures of base-10 blocks to complete the table.

Rule
Add 12

In	Out	Out in a Different Way
▪▪▪	| ▪▪▪▪▪	▪▪▪▪▪ ▪▪▪▪▪
|	|| ▪▪	
|| ▪▪▪▪	*1110000*	
|| ▪▪▪▪▪ ▪		

2. Write the rule. Then complete the table.

Rule

In	Out	Out in a Different Way
||||| ▪▪▪	||||| ▪▪▪▪▪ ▪▪▪▪	||||| ▪▪▪▪▪ ▪▪▪▪▪
| ▪▪▪▪▪▪ ▪▪	|| ▪▪▪▪▪ ▪▪▪▪▪	| ▪▪▪▪▪▪▪ ▪▪▪▪▪
||||| ▪		
▪▪▪▪▪		

Pockets Bar Graph

Family Note

Help your child to first fill in the table below and then display the data by making a **bar graph.**

Please return this Home Link to school tomorrow.

1. Pick five people. Count the number of pockets that each person's clothing has. Complete the table.

Name	Number of Pockets

2. Draw a bar graph for your data. First, write the name of each person on a line at the bottom of the graph. Then, color the bar above each name to show how many pockets that person has.

How Many Pockets

Number of Pockets

8+
7
6
5
4
3
2
1
0

Names

Frames-and-Arrows Problems

Family Note

Frames-and-Arrows diagrams show sequences of numbers—numbers that follow one after the other according to a rule.

The problems on this Home Link are a variation of the Frames-and-Arrows problems your child brought home in the last unit. In each of the problems below, two different rules are represented by two different arrows.

Please return this Home Link to school tomorrow.

Show someone at home how to solve these Frames-and-Arrows problems. Use coins to help you.

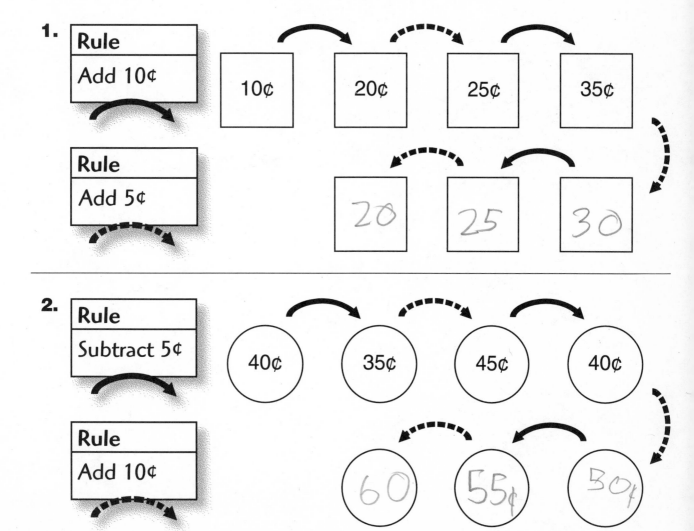

Counting up to Make Change

Family Note

Help your child identify the amount of change that he or she would receive by "counting up" from the price of the item to the amount of money that was used to pay for the item. It may be helpful to act out the problems with your child using real coins and bills.

Please return this Home Link to school tomorrow.

Complete the table.

I buy:	It costs:	I pay with:	My change is:
a bag of potato chips	70¢	Q Q Q	_____ ¢
a box of crayons	65¢	$1	_____ ¢
a pen	59¢	Q Q Q	_____ ¢
an apple	45¢	D D D D D	_____ ¢
a notebook	73¢	Q Q D D N	_____ ¢
a ruler	48¢	$1	_____ ¢
			_____ ¢
			_____ ¢

Family Letter

Unit 4: Addition and Subtraction

In Unit 4, children will use addition and subtraction stories to develop mental-arithmetic skills. Mental arithmetic is computation done in one's head or by drawing pictures, making tallies, or using manipulatives (counters, money, number lines, and number grids—no calculators, though). Children can also use their own solution strategies.

A second grader uses a number grid to solve 5 + 9.

1	2	3	4	⑤	6	7	8	9	10
11	12	13	⑭	⑮	16	17	18	19	20
21	22	23	24	25	26	27	28	29	30

I started at 5 and jumped ahead 10 to 15. But the problem said to add only 9, so I moved back 1 to 14.

Addition has two basic meanings: *putting together* and *changing to more*. In this unit, children will use **parts-and-total diagrams** and **change diagrams** to help them organize information in addition stories that either "put together" or "change to more." See the vocabulary section on page 276 to learn more about these diagrams.

Parts-and-Total Diagram

Total	
?	
Part	Part
20	16

Change Diagram

Start	Change	End
20	+6	?

Children will also develop estimation skills by solving problems that involve purchases. For example, your child will estimate whether $5.00 is enough to buy a pen that costs $1.69, a notebook that costs $2.25, and a ruler that costs 89¢.

In the last part of this unit, children will learn paper-and-pencil strategies for addition and will continue to gain hands-on experience with thermometers, money, tape measures, and rulers. Home Links 4.8 and 4.9, which you will receive later, will give you more information on the paper-and-pencil strategies that your child will be learning.

Please keep this Family Letter for reference as your child works through Unit 4.

Vocabulary

Important terms in Unit 4:

change-to-more number story A number story having a starting quantity that is increased so that the ending quantity is more than the starting quantity.

For example: *Nick has 20 comic books. He buys 6 more. How many comic books does Nick have now?*

change diagram A device used to organize information in a change-to-more or change-to-less number story. The change diagram below illustrates the above change-to-more number story.

Start	Change	End
20	+6	?

mental arithmetic Computation done totally or partially in one's head, using a variety of strategies.

parts-and-total number story A number story in which two or more quantities (parts) are combined to form a total quantity. For example: *Carl baked 20 cookies. Sam baked 16 cookies. How many cookies did Carl and Sam bake in all?*

parts-and-total diagram A device used to organize information in a parts-and-total number story. The parts-and-total diagram below, for example, illustrates the previous example described under "parts-and-total number story."

Total	
?	
Part	**Part**
20	16

estimate An educated guess, or an answer in the right "ballpark," rather than an exact answer.

algorithm A step-by-step set of instructions for doing something—for example, for solving addition or subtraction problems.

Building Skills through Games

In Unit 4, your child will practice addition skills by playing the following game:

Addition Spin
A "Spinner" and a "Checker" take turns adding two numbers and checking the sum. After five turns, each player uses a calculator to find the sum of his or her scores. The player with the higher total wins!

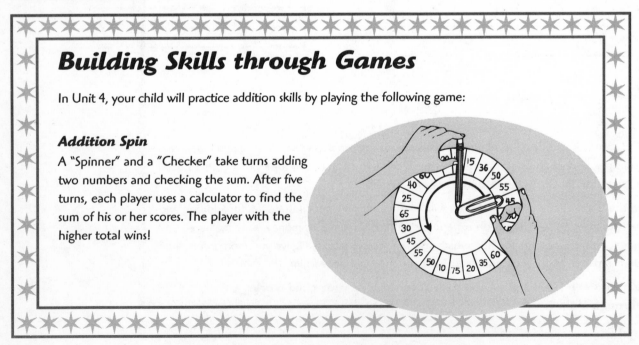

Use with Lesson 3.9.

Do-Anytime Activities

To work with your child on the concepts taught in this unit and in previous units, try these interesting and rewarding activities:

1 Encourage your child to show you addition and subtraction strategies as these are developed during the unit.

2 Make up number stories involving estimation. For example, pretend that your child has $2.00 and that he or she wants to buy a pencil marked 64¢, a tablet marked 98¢, and an eraser marked 29¢. Help your child to estimate the total cost of the three items (without tax) and to determine if there is enough money to buy them. If appropriate, you can also ask your child to estimate the amount of change due.

3 Look at weather reports in the newspaper and on television and discuss differences between high and low temperatures. Also note the differences between the Fahrenheit and Celsius scales.

As You Help Your Child with Homework

As your child brings home assignments, you may want to go over the instructions together, clarifying them as necessary. The answers listed below will guide you through this unit's Home Links.

Home Link 4.1

1. 18 grapes; 11 + 7 = 18

2. 38 cards; 30 + 8 = 38

3. 52 pounds; 42 + 10 = 52

4. 27   **5.** 80   **6.** 83

7. 10   **8.** 17   **9.** 70

10. 30   **11.** 66   **12.** 80

Home Link 4.2

1. 47 pounds; 17 + 30 = 47

2. 75 pounds; 45 + 30 = 75

3. 60 pounds; 15 + 45 = 60

4. 92 pounds; 17 + 45 + 30 = 92

Home Link 4.3

Home Link 4.4

1. 20°F   **2.** 34°F   **3.** 52°F

4. 96°F   **5.** 48°F   **6.** 73°F

13. 70   **14.** 35   **15.** 97

16. 26   **17.** 50   **18.** 68

Home Link 4.5

1. no   **2.** yes   **3.** no   **4.** yes

5. 100   **6.** 46   **7.** 47

Home Link 4.6

1. 30 marbles; 20 + 10 = 30

2. 54 cookies; 30 + 24 = 54

3. 100   **4.** 140   **5.** 79   **6.** 83

7. 94   **8.** 77

Home Link 4.7

2. About 20 inches

Home Link 4.8

1. 76   **2.** 100   **3.** 83   **4.** 120

5. 98   **6.** 90   **7.** 93   **8.** 85

9. 71   **10.** 83   **11.** 169   **12.** 544

Home Link 4.9

1. 89   **2.** 108   **3.** 83   **4.** 94

5. 77   **6.** 92   **7.** 185   **8.** 363

Reading a Thermometer

Family Note

In today's lesson, your child read temperatures on a real thermometer and on a thermometer pictured on a poster. The thermometers on this page show three different-size degree marks. The longest marks show 10-degree intervals, the medium-size marks show even-number degree intervals, and the shortest marks show odd-number degree intervals.

Help your child find the temperature shown by each thermometer by starting at a degree mark showing tens, counting the medium-size marks by 2s, and, if the temperature is at a short mark, counting 1 more.

Please return this Home Link to school tomorrow.

Circle the thermometer that shows the correct temperature.

1. 40°F

2. 82°F

3. 10°C

4. 3°C

Temperature

Family Note

In today's lesson, your child solved problems involving temperatures. On the thermometers on this Home Link, the longer degree marks are spaced at 2-degree intervals. Point to these degree marks while your child counts by 2s; "40, 42, 44, 46, 48, 50 degrees."

Problems 6 and 12 involve temperatures that are an "odd" number of degrees. Help your child use the shorter degree marks to get the correct answers.

Please return this Home Link to school tomorrow.

Write the temperature shown on each thermometer.

1.

_____

2.

_____

3. 60

_____

4. 110

_____

5.

_____

6. 80

_____

Temperature (cont.)

Home Link 4.4

Fill in each thermometer to show the temperature.

7. Show 44°F.

8. Show 102°F.

9. Show 60°F.

10. Show 56°F.

11. Show 38°F.

12. Show 27°F.

Add or subtract.

13. $30 + 40 = $ _____

14. $75 - 40 = $ _____

15. _____ $= 7 + 90$

16. _____ $= 46 - 20$

17.   53
    −   3

18.   60
    +   8

Use with Lesson 4.4.

Name _____ Date _____ Time _____

Shopping at the Grocery Store

 Family Note

Many problems in and out of the classroom require estimates rather than exact answers. In Problems 1–5 below, you need to know only whether the total cost is greater than $1.00 or less than $1.00; you do not need to know the exact total cost. In Problem 1, for example, help your child notice that the price of the can of frozen orange juice (98¢) is almost $1.00. Since a lemon is 10¢, your child could not buy both items.

Please return this Home Link to school tomorrow.

You have $1.00 to spend at the grocery store. Use estimation to answer each question.

Can you buy: **Circle *Yes* or *No*.**

1. a can of frozen orange juice and a lemon?   Yes   No

2. a banana and a dozen eggs?   Yes   No

3. a container of yogurt and a roll of paper towels?   Yes   No

4. a lemon and a can of soup?   Yes   No

Add or subtract.

5. 50 + 50 = _____   **6.** _____ = 6 + 40   **7.** _____ = 67 − 20

Addition Number Stories

Family Note

In today's lesson, your child solved problems by adding 2-digit numbers mentally. For example, to find $34 + 23$, you might first add the tens: $30 + 20 = 50$. Then add the ones: $4 + 3 = 7$. Finally, combine the tens and ones: $50 + 7 = 57$.

Please return this Home Link to school tomorrow.

Try to solve Problems 1 and 2 mentally. Fill in the diagrams. Then write the answers and number models.

1. Ruth had 20 marbles in her collection. Her brother gave her 10 more. How many marbles does Ruth have now?

Start	Change	End
20	10	30

Answer: _____30_____
   (unit)

Number model:

_____20 + 10 = 30_____

2. Tim baked 30 ginger snaps and 24 sugar cookies. How many cookies did he bake?

Total	
54	
Part	**Part**
30	24

Answer: _____54_____
   (unit)

Number model:

_____30 + 24 = 54_____

Try to do each problem mentally. Then write the answer.

Unit
raisins

3. _____ = 40 + 60

4. 90 + 50 = _____

5. _____ = 70 + 9

6. 80 + 3 = _____

7. 30 + 64 = _____

8. _____ = 27 + 50

Addition Strategies

Family Note

Everyday Mathematics encourages children to use a variety of strategies to solve computation problems. By doing so, children are developing a sense for numbers and operations rather than simply memorizing a series of steps.

We suggest that you give your child an opportunity to explore and choose addition strategies that he or she feels comfortable using. At some point, you may want to share the method that you know from your own school experience. But please allow your child some time to use his or her own methods before doing so.

Below are three examples of methods that your child might use to solve 2-digit addition problems.

Counting On

$47 + 33 = ?$ ◄───── "My problem"

47 57 67 77   ◄───── "Start at 47. Count up 30 more."

$\underline{+ \ 3}$ ◄───── "Add on 3 more."

80   ◄───── "The answer is 80."

Combining Groups (1s, 10s, ...) Separately

$29 + 37 = ?$ ◄───── "My problem"

$20 + 30 = 50$ ◄───── "Add the tens."

$9 + 7 = \underline{16}$ ◄───── "Add the ones."

66   ◄───── "Put these together. The answer is 66."

Adjusting and Compensating

$52 + 29 = ?$ ◄───── "My problem"

30   ◄───── "30 is close to 29, just 1 more."

$52 + 30 = 82$ ◄───── "52 plus 30 is 82."

$\underline{- \ 1}$ ◄───── "Take away 1, because I added 30 instead of 29."

81   ◄───── "The answer is 81."

Encourage your child to use a "ballpark estimate" as a way to check whether or not an answer to a computation problem makes sense. For example, in $34 + 59$, 34 is close to 30 and 59 is close to 60. $30 + 60 = 90$ is your ballpark estimate. "90 is close to my answer 93, so 93 is a reasonable answer."

*Please return the **second page** of this Home Link to school tomorrow.*

Addition Strategies (cont.)

**Home Link
4.8**

Add.

1. $40 + 36 = \underline{76}$ **2.** $20 + 80 = \underline{100}$ **3.** $\underline{83} = 53 + 30$

4. $60 + 60 = \underline{120}$ **5.** $\underline{98} = 50 + 48$ **6.** $\underline{90} = 70 + 20$

Add. Show your work in the workspaces.

Check your work. Write a number model to show your ballpark estimate.

7.
$$\begin{array}{r} 34 \\ + 59 \\ \hline \end{array}$$

_33_ _60_ _90_

Answer

Ballpark estimate:

$30 + 60 = 90$

8. $17 + 68$

_715_

Answer

Ballpark estimate:

9. $46 + 25$

Answer

Ballpark estimate:

_____

10. $56 + 27$

Answer

Ballpark estimate:

_____

11. $123 + 46$

Answer

Ballpark estimate:

_____

12.
$$\begin{array}{r} 318 \\ + 226 \\ \hline \end{array}$$

Answer

Ballpark estimate:

_____

Unit 5: 3-D and 2-D Shapes

Geometry is an important component of *Everyday Mathematics*. Studying geometry helps develop spatial sense and the ability to represent and describe the world. Instead of waiting until ninth or tenth grade, *Everyday Mathematics* introduces geometric fundamentals in Kindergarten and develops them over time. Children are thus prepared to study more advanced geometric topics later.

In Unit 5, children will consider five basic kinds of 3-dimensional shapes: prisms, pyramids, cylinders, cones, and spheres. To sort the shapes, children will explore similarities and differences among them. They will become familiar with both the names of shapes and the terms for parts of shapes.

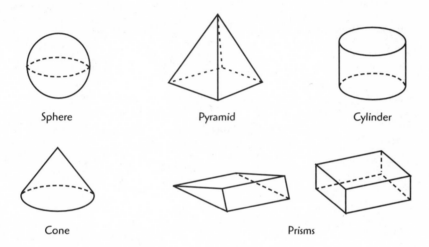

Sphere   Pyramid   Cylinder

Cone   Prisms

Children will also study **polygons,** or 2-dimensional shapes that form the flat surfaces of prisms and pyramids, as they look for examples in real life.

Later in the unit, children will explore **line symmetry** as they experiment with folding 2-dimensional shapes and matching the halves. Children will also cut out shapes and look for lines of symmetry in each shape. When children are given half of a shape, they will draw the missing half. Children will be asked to find symmetrical objects at home and in other places.

Please keep this Family Letter for reference as your child works through Unit 5.

Vocabulary

The purpose of introducing children to the various shapes is to explore the characteristics of the shapes, not to teach vocabulary. This list is presented simply to acquaint you with some of the terms your child will be hearing in context in the classroom.

line segment Part of a straight line connecting two points.

Line segment *AB* or *BA*

angle (of a polygon) A figure formed by any two sides that have a common endpoint.

parallel Always the same distance apart; never meeting.

Two parallel lines

polygon A 2-dimensional figure with straight sides (line segments) connected end to end and no side crosses another side. *Poly-* means *many*, and *-gon* means *angle*.

polyhedron A 3-dimensional geometric shape with flat surfaces. The following shapes are regular polyhedrons:

Tetrahedron   Cube   Octahedron

Dodecahedron   Icosahedron

face A flat surface on a 3-dimensional shape.

faces

vertex (corner) The point at which the sides of a polygon meet; the point at which the edges of a polyhedron meet.

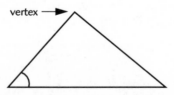

vertex

line symmetry The exact matching of two halves of a shape.

Use with Lesson 4.10.

Do-Anytime Activities

To work with your child on the concepts taught in this unit and in previous units, try these interesting and rewarding activities:

1 Together, look for 2-dimensional and 3-dimensional shapes in your home and neighborhood. Explore and name shapes and brainstorm about their characteristics. For example, compare a soup can and a tissue box. Talk about the differences between the shapes of the surfaces.

2 Use household items, such as toothpicks and marshmallows, straws and twist-ties, sticks, and paper to construct shapes like those shown below.

3 Look for geometric patterns in tile floors, quilts, buildings, and so on.

Use with Lesson 4.10.

As You Help Your Child with Homework

As your child brings home assignments, you may want to go over the instructions together, clarifying them as necessary. The answers listed below will guide you through this unit's Home Links.

1.

2. The shapes all have 4 sides.

1.   **2.**   **3.**

1.   **2.**   **3.**

6 triangles

1.   **2.** 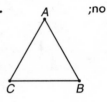   ;no

1. the trapezoid   **2.** the square

3. the rectangle

Building Skills through Games

In Unit 5, your child will practice addition, time-telling, and money skills by playing the following games:

Addition Spin

Players "spin the wheel" twice and add the two selected numbers. Players check their partners' addition with a calculator.

Dollar Rummy

Instead of three-of-a-kind, players look for two cards that will add up to $1.00.

Clock Concentration

Players match pairs of cards showing the time on analog and digital clocks, or with words.

Name _____ Date _____ Time _____

Family Note

Your child has been classifying shapes according to such rules as *only large shapes*, *only small red shapes*, or *only triangles*. Help your child determine which shapes in Problem 1 fit the rule by checking those shapes against the shapes below. What do all of the shapes that fit the rule have in common? (They all have 4 sides.) Once your child thinks that she or he knows the rule, check that rule against the shapes that do NOT fit the rule. Do any of those shapes follow the proposed rule?

Please return this Home Link to school tomorrow.

These shapes fit the rule.

These shapes do NOT fit the rule.

---

1. Which of these shapes fit the rule? Circle them.

2. What is the rule? _____

3. Draw a new shape that fits the rule.

Polygons

Family Note

In this lesson, your child has been learning the names of different polygons. A polygon is a closed figure made up of straight sides, and you can trace and come back to where you started without retracing or crossing any part. Different types of polygons are shown below. Examples of polygons can be found in real-life objects. For example, a stop sign is an octagon and this page is a rectangle. As your child cuts out pictures of polygons, discuss each shape. Count the sides and angles and try to name the polygons. Talk about how the polygons are alike and different.

Please return this Home Link to school tomorrow or as requested by the teacher.

1. Cut out pictures from newspapers and magazines that show triangles, quadrangles, and other polygons. Ask an adult for permission first.

2. Paste each picture on a sheet of paper.

3. Write the names of some of the polygons under the pictures.

4. Bring your pictures to school.

Triangles	**Quadrangles or Quadrilaterals**
Pentagons	**Hexagons**
Heptagons	**Octagons**

These are NOT polygons.

Line Segments

Family Note

In this lesson, your child learned to name points and line segments with capital letters. Using a straightedge, your child drew line segments to create shapes. Provide your child with a ruler, a piece of stiff cardboard, or another object having a straight edge. Observe as your child draws line segments. Ask your child to name the shapes that he or she draws in Problems 1 and 2 below (a 6-pointed star and a hexagon).

Please return this Home Link to school tomorrow.

Use a straightedge to draw line segments.

1. Draw these line segments:

$\overline{AC}$

$\overline{CE}$

$\overline{EA}$

$\overline{BF}$

$\overline{BD}$

$\overline{DF}$

A
B   F
C   D   E

2. Draw these line segments:

$\overline{AB}$

$\overline{BC}$

$\overline{CD}$

$\overline{DE}$

$\overline{EF}$

$\overline{FA}$

A
B   F
C   D   E

3. Draw the following line segments:

$\overline{AB}$, $\overline{BC}$

$\overline{CD}$, $\overline{DE}$

$\overline{EF}$, $\overline{FA}$

$\overline{AD}$, $\overline{FC}$

$\overline{BE}$

B
A   C
F   E   D

How many triangles are

there? _____

4. Draw points on the back of this page. Label each point with a letter. Use a straightedge to connect the points with line segments to make polygons.

Parallel Line Segments

1. Draw line segments *AB, BC, CD,* and *DA.*

$A\bullet$ $\bullet B$

Put a red **X** on the line segment that is parallel to line segment *AB.*

Put a blue **X** on the line segment that is parallel to line segment *BC.*

$D\bullet$ $\bullet C$

2. Draw line segments *AB, BC,* and *CA.*

A
$\bullet$

Is any line segment in your drawing parallel to line segment *AB*? _____

$C\bullet$ $\bullet B$

Special Family Note

In Lesson 5.7, your child will be studying 3-dimensional shapes. Help your child gather 3-dimensional objects for a class collection that we call the "Shapes Museum." You and your child might want to separate the objects you collect according to shape.

Shapes Museum

For the next few days, your class will collect things to put into a Shapes Museum. Starting tomorrow, bring items like boxes, soup cans, party hats, pyramids, and balls to school. Ask an adult for permission before bringing in these items. Make sure that the things you bring are clean.

Graphing Data

Family Note

The class has been collecting and graphing data about favorite foods. Ask your child about the graph he or she made in class. In the table below, help your child count the tally marks below the name of each fruit. To decide how high up to color each bar, your child could lay a straightedge across the columns.

Please return this Home Link to school tomorrow.

In a survey, people were asked to name their favorite fruit. The table below shows the results.

apple	watermelon	pear	banana	grapes
ⵌ	ⵌ ///	///	////	ⵌ ⵌ

1. Make a bar graph that shows how many people chose each fruit. The first bar has been colored for you.

Favorite Fruits

2. Which fruit is the most popular? _____

Which fruit is the least popular? _____

What is your favorite kind of fruit? _____

Number Stories and Diagrams

Family Note

In today's lesson, your child used diagrams to solve number stories. Listen to your child's stories. Ask your child to explain how each story relates to both the diagram and the number model. (See Home Link 5.10: *Unit 6 Family Letter* for information about number stories and diagrams.)

Please return this Home Link to school tomorrow.

Write number stories to match each diagram. Then finish the number model. Tell your stories to someone at home.

1.

Unit
building blocks

Start	Change	End
24	+6	?

_____

_____

Finish the number model: 24 + 6 = _____

2.

Unit
books

Total	
Part	Part

_____

_____

Finish the number model: 15 + 13 = _____

Stories and Diagrams (cont.)

3.

Unit
bananas

Quantity

Quantity	Difference

_____

_____

Finish the number model: 28 − 8 = _____

4.

Unit
baseball cards

Total	
Part	Part

_____

_____

Write a number model for your story.

Number model: _____

Trade-First Subtraction

Family Note

Today your child learned about subtracting multidigit numbers using a procedure called the trade-first method. Your child also used "ballpark estimates" to determine whether or not his or her answers made sense.

The **trade-first** method is similar to the traditional subtraction method that you may be familiar with. However, all of the "regrouping" or "borrowing" is done before the problem is solved—which gives the method its name, "trade-first."

Example

longs 10s	cubes 1s
4	6
−3	9

· Are there enough tens and ones to remove exactly 3 tens and 9 ones from 46? (*No; there are enough tens, but there aren't enough ones.*)

· Trade 1 ten for 10 ones.

longs 10s	cubes 1s
3	1̸6
4̸	6̸
−3	9
5	7

· Solve. 3 tens minus 3 tens leaves 0 tens. 16 ones minus 9 ones leaves 7 ones. The answer is 7.

longs 10s	cubes 1s
3	1 6
4̸	6̸
−3	9
	7

· Make a ballpark estimate to see whether the answer makes sense: 46 is close to 50, and 39 is close to 40. 50 − 40 = 10. 10 is close to the answer of 7, so 7 is a reasonable answer.

The trade-first method is one of many ways people solve subtraction problems. Your child may choose this method or may prefer to use a different procedure. What is most important is that your child can successfully solve subtraction problems using a method that makes sense to him or her.

*Please return the **second page** of this Home Link to school tomorrow.*

Name   Date   Time

Trade-First Subtraction (cont.)

Make a ballpark estimate for each problem and write a number model for your estimate.

Use the trade-first method of subtraction to solve each problem.

Example:

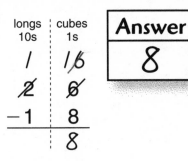

longs 10s	cubes 1s
1	1̸6̸
2̸	6̸
−1	8
	8

Answer 8

Ballpark estimate:

$$30 - 20 = 10$$

1.

longs 10s	cubes 1s
7	3
−4	2

Answer

Ballpark estimate:

_____

2.

longs 10s	cubes 1s
4	9
−2	6

Answer

Ballpark estimate:

_____

3.

longs 10s	cubes 1s
8	5
−5	6

Answer

Ballpark estimate:

_____

4.

longs 10s	cubes 1s
3	2
−1	5

Answer

Ballpark estimate:

_____

5. 34 − 18

Answer

Ballpark estimate:

_____

How Many?

Family Note

Your child has been working with arrays—rectangular arrangements of objects having the same number of objects in each row—to develop readiness for multiplication. Since this is a readiness activity, children have not yet written number models for multiplication, such as $4 \times 5 = 20$. Your child will do this in later lessons in this unit.

Please return this Home Link to school tomorrow.

1. Show someone at home this array.

X X X X X
X X X X X
X X X X X
X X X X X

How many rows? _____

How many **X**s in each row? _____

How many **X**s in all? _____

2. Draw an array of 16 **X**s.

How many rows? _____

How many **X**s in each row? _____

3. Draw an array of 24 **X**s.

How many rows? _____

How many **X**s in each row? _____

4. Draw a different array of 24 **X**s.

How many rows? _____

How many **X**s in each row? _____

How Many?

Family Note

In today's lesson, your child learned that multiplication is an operation used to find the total number of things in several equal groups. As you help your child solve the following problems, emphasize that each group has the same number of things. Your child can use objects, draw pictures, count, or use any other helpful devices to find the answers.

Please return this Home Link to school tomorrow.

Example

How many apples in 4 packages?

|||| |||| |||| ||||

$5 + 5 + 5 + 5 = 20$

There are 20 apples in 4 packages.

1. △ △ △ △ △ △

How many sides on each triangle? _____ sides

How many sides in all? _____ sides

2.

How many tires on each car? _____ tires

How many tires in all? _____ tires

3.

How many fingers for each person?

_____ fingers

How many fingers in all?

_____ fingers

Arrays

Family Note

In this lesson, your child solved multiplication problems about arrays, which are rectangular arrangements of objects in rows and columns. Encourage your child to use counters, such as pennies or buttons, while working on the following exercises.

Please return this Home Link to school tomorrow.

Tell someone at home what you know about arrays.

1. Look at the array and fill in the blank. • 4 rows of dots 6 dots in each row _____ dots in all	**2.** Draw an array of dots. Your array should have 5 rows of dots 7 dots in each row That's _____ dots in all.	**3.** Draw an array of 12 dots.

Telephone:
a 4-by-3 array

Muffins:
a 3-by-2 array

Muffins:
a 4-by-3 array

Tic-tac-toe Grid:
a 3-by-3 array

Checkerboard:
an 8-by-8 array

Eggs:
a 2-by-6 array

Arrays

Family Note

In this lesson, your child continued to work with arrays to develop multiplication concepts. Your child described each array by naming the number of rows, the number of items in each row, and the total number of items in the array. Your child wrote number models to describe arrays. In the example, an array with 2 rows of 4 dots can be described using the number model 2 × 4 = 8.

Please return this Home Link to school tomorrow.

Show an array for the numbers that are given. Find the total number of dots in the array. Complete the number model.

Example

Numbers: 2, 4

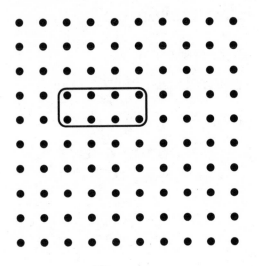

Total: __8__

Number model:

__2__ × __4__ = __8__

1. Numbers: 7, 3

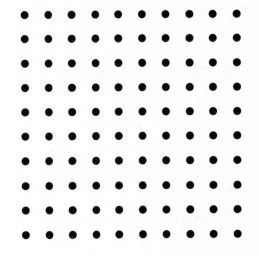

Total: _____

Number model:

_____ × _____ = _____

Arrays (cont.)

2. Numbers: 6, 10

Total: _____

Number model:

_____ × _____ = _____

_____

Answer the questions about each array.

3.

How many rows? _____

How many
dots in each row? _____

How many
dots in the array? _____

4.

How many rows? _____

How many
squares per row? _____

How many
squares in the array? _____

5.

How many rows? _____

How many squares in each row? _____

How many squares in the array? _____

Use with Lesson 6.10.

Division

Family Note

In this lesson, your child worked on the concept of division by putting objects into equal groups and sharing objects equally among several people. Objects that are left over are called the *remainder*. If 9 books are shared equally among 4 people, each person gets 2 books, and the 1 book that is left over is the remainder.

Watch as your child divides things equally among family members. Try to use groups of objects that can be divided with no remainder as well as groups that have remainders.

Please return this Home Link to school tomorrow.

1. Have someone at home give you a group or handful of small items, such as raisins, buttons, or popcorn. Show how you can divide the items equally among your family members. Are any items left over?

Make a record of what you did. Be ready to tell about it in class.

I shared _____ (how many?) items equally among _____ people.

Each person got _____. There were _____ left over.

2. Do this again with some other kind of item.

I shared _____ items equally among _____ people.

Each person got _____. There were _____ left over.

3. 19 cents shared equally

by 2 people   by 3 people   by 4 people

_____¢ per person _____¢ per person _____¢ per person

_____¢ remaining _____¢ remaining _____¢ remaining

Family Letter

Unit 7: **Patterns and Rules**

In Unit 7, children will concentrate on number patterns, computational skills, and the application of mathematics through the use of data. They will continue to use the 100-grid as a means of reinforcing numeration skills. Children will also explore the patterns of doubling and halving numbers, which will help prepare them for multiplication and division.

Computational work will be extended to several 2-digit numbers and to the subtraction of 1- and 2-digit numbers from multiples of 10.

Children will learn to find complements of tens; that is, they will answer such questions as "What must I add to 4 to get to 10? What must I add to 47 to get to 50?" or "How many tens are needed to get from 320 to 400?"

Children will also collect and interpret real-life data about animals, adults, and themselves. For example, they will collect data by measuring the lengths of their standing long jumps and then find the median jump length for the class.

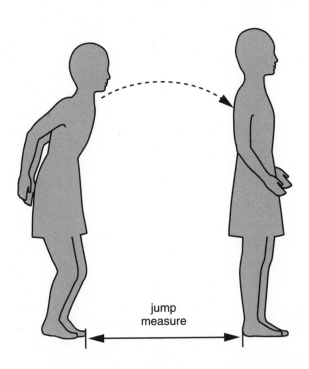

jump
measure

Please keep this Family Letter for reference as your child works through Unit 7.

Vocabulary

Important terms in Unit 7:

arrow-path puzzles Pieces of the number grid used to reinforce the structure of our base-ten numeration system.

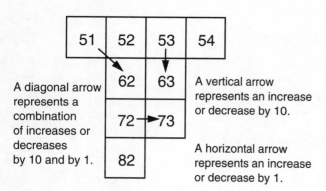

A diagonal arrow represents a combination of increases or decreases by 10 and by 1.

A vertical arrow represents an increase or decrease by 10.

A horizontal arrow represents an increase or decrease by 1.

median The number in the middle when a set of data is organized in sequential order; also called the *middle value*. For example, in the set of data below, 35 is the median.

30, 32, 32, 35, 36, 38, 40

frequency The number of times an event or value occurs in a set of data. For example, in the set of data above, 32 has a frequency of 2.

Do-Anytime Activities

To work with your child on the concepts taught in this unit and in previous units, try these interesting and rewarding activities:

1 If you have a calculator at home, practice making (and breaking) tens.

For example:

Making tens: Enter 33. What needs to be done to display 50? $33 +$ _____ $= 50$

Breaking tens: Enter 60. What needs to be done to display 52? $60 -$ _____ $= 52$

Or, for more challenging practice, try the following:

Enter 27. What needs to be done to display 40?

Enter 90. What needs to be done to display 66?

Try other similar numbers.

2 Make a game out of doubling, tripling, and quadrupling small numbers. For example, using the number 2, first double it. What number do you get? Continue the doubling process five more times. Then start again with the number 2 and triple it; then quadruple it. Discuss the differences among the final numbers.

3 Collect a simple set of data from family and friends. For example, how high can different people's fingertips reach while the people are standing flat on the floor? Order the data to find the median.

Use with Lesson 6.12.

Building Skills through Games

In Unit 7, your child will practice addition and subtraction skills by playing the following games:

Array Bingo

Players roll the dice and find an *Array Bingo* card with the same number of dots. Players then turn that card over. The first player to have a row, column, or diagonal of facedown cards calls out "Bingo!" and wins the game.

Hit the Target

Players choose a 2-digit multiple of ten as a "target number." One player enters a "starting number" on a calculator and tries to change the starting number to the target number by adding a number to it on the calculator. Children practice finding differences between 2-digit numbers and higher multiples of tens.

Use with Lesson 6.12.

As You Help Your Child with Homework

As your child brings home assignments, you may want to go over the instructions together, clarifying them as necessary. The answers listed below will guide you through this unit's Home Links.

Home Link 7.3

1. 6; 7; 5; 9; 2   **2.** 6; 7; 5; 9; 8

3. 32 + 38; 65 + 5; 10 + 60; 43 + 27; 19 + 51; 51 + 19; 27 + 43

Home Link 7.4

1. Team A: 35; Team B: 25; A

2. Team A: 30; Team B: 35; B

3. Team A: 29; Team B: 40; B

4. Team A: 45; Team B: 59; B

Home Link 7.5

1.

in	out
12	6
50	25
40	20
30	15
16	8
18	9

in → Rule Half → out

2. 1, 2, 4, 8, 16, 32, 64

3. 3, 6, 12, 24, 48, 96, 192

4. 127 pennies, or $1.27

Home Link 7.6

1. 8 pounds **2.** 20 pounds **3.** 5 pounds

4. 65 pounds **5.** 11,000 pounds

Home Link 7.7

1. 13 centimeters   **2.** 2 inches

3. 3 inches   **4.** 17 centimeters

5. 9 centimeters

Home Link 7.8

1. 3   7   9   (12)   15   20   21
     points points points points points points points

2. 56 in. 66 in. (68 in.) 70 in. 73 in.

3. 142 cm 168 cm (173 cm) 178 cm 185 cm

Home Link 7.9

1. 2   **2.** 0   **3.** 46   **4.** 52

5. 9   **6.** 48   **7.** 49

Number-Grid Puzzle

Family Note

In this lesson, your child solved a special type of puzzle called a *number-grid puzzle*. Solving number-grid puzzles promotes place-value awareness that will help your child develop addition and subtraction skills. In the number grid shown below, the numbering starts at 100, and then the numbers increase by 1 as you move from left to right in each row. The shaded cells of the number grid should not be filled in. However, if your child is having difficulty, you might fill in a few of the shaded cells to provide some additional clues.

Please return this Home Link to school tomorrow.

Fill in the blank (unshaded) cells of the number grid.

									100
101	102								

Missing Addends

Family Note

In this lesson, your child found the difference between a number and a multiple of 10. In Problems 1 and 2, your child will find the difference between a number and the next-higher multiple of 10. For example, your child will determine which number added to 62 equals 70 (8). In Problem 3, your child will find different combinations of numbers that add to 70. If your child has difficulty with this problem, suggest changing the first number in each combination to the next-higher multiple of 10. For example, add 2 to 48 to make 50 and then add 20 to 50 to make 70. $2 + 20 = 22$, so $48 + 22 = 70$.

Please return this Home Link to school tomorrow.

---

1. $4 + \underline{\hspace{1.5cm}} = 10$

$10 = 3 + \underline{\hspace{1.5cm}}$

$\underline{\hspace{1.5cm}} + 5 = 10$

$10 = \underline{\hspace{1.5cm}} + 1$

$8 + \underline{\hspace{1.5cm}} = 10$

2. $54 + \underline{\hspace{1.5cm}} = 60$

$90 = 83 + \underline{\hspace{1.5cm}}$

$75 + \underline{\hspace{1.5cm}} = 80$

$40 = 31 + \underline{\hspace{1.5cm}}$

$\underline{\hspace{1.5cm}} + 62 = 70$

---

3. Make 70s. Show someone at home how you did it.

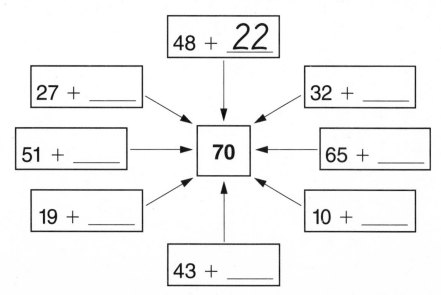

Who Scored More Points?

Home Link 7.4

Family Note

In this lesson, your child added three or more 1-digit and 2-digit numbers. As your child completes the problems below, encourage him or her to share the different ways in which the points can be added. Your child might add all of the tens first and then add all of the ones. For example, $20 + 5 + 4 + 6 = 20 + 15 = 35$. Your child may also look for combinations of numbers that are easier to add. In Game 1, for example, first add 14 and 6 to get 20 and then add 15 to get 35.

Please return this Home Link to school tomorrow.

Do the following for each problem:

Unit
points

• Add the points for each team.

• Decide which team scored more points. The team with the greater number of points wins the game.

• Circle your answer.

1. Game 1

Team A:
$15 + 14 + 6 =$ _____

Team B:
$5 + 13 + 7 =$ _____

Who won? A or B

2. Game 2

Team A:
$12 + 6 + 4 + 8 =$ _____

Team B:
$5 + 10 + 19 + 1 =$ _____

Who won? A or B

3. Game 3

Team A:
$17 + 4 + 5 + 3 =$ _____

Team B:
$2 + 11 + 9 + 18 =$ _____

Who won? A or B

4. Game 4

Team A:
$7 + 4 + 16 + 13 + 5 =$ _____

Team B:
$22 + 9 + 8 + 3 + 17 =$ _____

Who won? A or B

Doubles and Halves

Family Note

In today's lesson, your child heard a story and used a calculator to double numbers and find halves of numbers repeatedly. Help your child solve the doubling and halving problems below. When appropriate, have your child use money or counters to help solve the problems. In Problem 1, for example, your child might display 40 counters, divide them into two equal groups, and then count to find that half of 40 is 20.

Please return this Home Link to school tomorrow.

1. Write a rule in the rule box.
Then complete the table.

in
↓

Rule

↓
out

in	out
12	6
50	25
40	
30	
	8
	9

2. Fill in the frames using the rule in the rule box.

Rule
Double

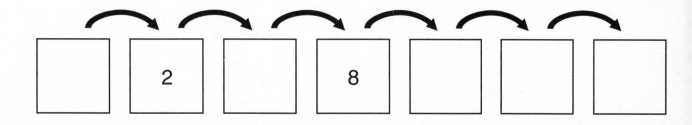

| | 2 | | 8 | | | |

Doubles and Halves (cont.)

3. Fill in the frames using the rule in the rule box.

Rule
Double

Challenge

4. Jay finds 1 penny under his pillow when he wakes up on Monday morning. On Tuesday, he finds 2 pennies. On Wednesday, he finds 4 pennies. So, on Wednesday, he has a total of 7 cents.

On Thursday, Friday, Saturday, and Sunday, Jay finds double the amount of money he found under his pillow the day before. How much money does Jay have on Sunday?

_____

Estimating Weights

Family Note

In today's lesson, your child practiced reading weights, in pounds, on a bath scale. One purpose of this activity is to improve your child's perception of weight so that he or she can make more realistic estimates of weights. To help develop your child's ability to read a bath scale, take every opportunity at home to use your bath scale to determine the weights of objects.

Please return this Home Link to school tomorrow.

Circle the best estimate for the weight of each object.

1. newborn baby

8 pounds

20 pounds

70 pounds

2. Thanksgiving turkey

$\frac{1}{2}$ pound

20 pounds

70 pounds

3. bag of apples

5 pounds

35 pounds

65 pounds

4. adult Golden Retriever

6 pounds

20 pounds

65 pounds

5. An adult bull African elephant
(the largest animal on land)

100 pounds

500 pounds

11,000 pounds

Line Segment Lengths

Family Note

In today's lesson, your child measured his or her standing long jump in centimeters and his or her arm span in inches. Help your child draw and measure each line segment below.

Please return this Home Link to school tomorrow.

Draw and measure line segments. If necessary, cut out and use the ruler at the bottom of the next page.

1. Draw a line segment that is 5 inches long.

Measure the segment to the nearest centimeter.

The segment is about _____ centimeters long.

2. Draw a line segment that is 5 centimeters long.

Measure the segment to the nearest inch.

The segment is about _____ inches long.

Line Segment Lengths (cont.)

3. Draw a line segment that is 8 centimeters long.

Measure the segment to the nearest inch.

The segment is about _____ inches long.

4. Draw a line segment that is $6\frac{1}{2}$ inches long.

Measure the segment to the nearest centimeter.

The segment is about _____ centimeters long.

5. Draw a line segment that is $3\frac{1}{2}$ inches long.

Measure the segment to the nearest centimeter.

The segment is about _____ centimeters long.

| 0 | 1 | 2 | 3 | 4 | 5 | 6 | 7 |

inches

centimeters

81 71 91 51 41 31 21 11 01 6 8 7 9 5 4 3 2 1 0

Use with Lesson 7.7.

Find the Middle Value

Family Note

In this lesson, your child has sorted data in order to find the median. *Median* is a term used for the middle value. To find the median of a set of data, arrange the data in ascending or descending order. Count from either end to the number in the middle. The middle value is the median. As your child finds the median in Problems 2 and 3, remind him or her that "in." is the abbreviation for inches and "cm" is the abbreviation for centimeters.

Please return this Home Link to school tomorrow.

List the data in order from smallest to largest.

Draw a circle around the median in your list.

1.

12 points	3 points	21 points	15 points	20 points	7 points	9 points

_____   _____   _____   _____   _____   _____   _____

points   points   points   points   points   points   points

smallest   **largest**

Find the Middle Value (cont.)

2.

Bob: 66 in. tall	Amy: 70 in. tall	Peter: 56 in. tall	Kate: 73 in. tall	Andy: 68 in. tall

_____ in.   _____ in.   _____ in.   _____ in.   _____ in.

smallest   **largest**

3.

Bob: 168 cm tall	Amy: 178 cm tall	Peter: 142 cm tall	Kate: 185 cm tall	Andy: 173 cm tall

_____ cm   _____ cm   _____ cm   _____ cm   _____ cm

smallest   **largest**

Interpreting Data

Family Note

Today your child represented data using a bar graph and a frequency table. The table below is called a *frequency table* because it shows how often different heights occurred. Help your child use the data to answer the questions. Remind your child that to find the median of a set of data, he or she should arrange the data in ascending or descending order and then count from either end to the number in the middle. The middle value is the median.

Please return this Home Link to school tomorrow.

Mr. Wilson is a basketball coach. He measured the height of each player. Then he made the data table shown below.

1. How many players are

50 inches tall? _____ players

2. How many players are

47 inches tall? _____ players

3. The shortest player is

_____ inches tall.

4. The tallest player is

_____ inches tall.

Players' Heights

Height (inches)	Number of Players
46	1
47	0
48	3
49	1
50	2
51	1
52	1

5. How many players did Mr. Wilson

measure? _____ players

6. Which height occurs most often? _____ inches

7. Find the middle (median) height. _____ inches

Family Letter

Unit 8: Fractions

In Unit 8, children will review and extend concepts of fractions. Specifically, they will recognize fractions as names for parts of a whole, or ONE.

Children will see that, as with whole numbers, many different fractions can name the same quantity. For example, $\frac{2}{4}$ and $\frac{6}{12}$ are both names for $\frac{1}{2}$.

Children will also explore relationships among fractions as they work with pattern-block shapes and Fraction Cards that show shaded regions.

$\boxed{\frac{1}{2}}$

$\frac{1}{4} + \frac{1}{4}$ $\frac{3}{6}$

$1 - \frac{1}{2}$ $\frac{5}{10}$

$1 \div 2$ $\frac{3}{4} - \frac{1}{4}$

$\boxed{\frac{1}{2}}$ $\boxed{\frac{1}{3}}$

Children use Fraction Cards to compare fractions by looking at the shaded areas.

Please keep this Family Letter for reference as your child works through Unit 8.

Vocabulary

Important terms in Unit 8:

fraction A number that names equal parts of a whole, or ONE.

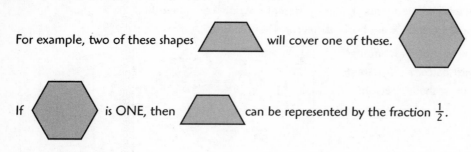

For example, two of these shapes   will cover one of these.

If   is ONE, then   can be represented by the fraction $\frac{1}{2}$.

denominator — The total number of equal parts into which the unit (or whole) is divided.	$\dfrac{3}{8}$	**numerator** — The number of equal parts of the unit (or whole) being considered.

It is not necessary for children to use the words numerator *and* denominator *now. They will learn them over time with repeated exposure. Do, however, use these words, as well as the informal "number on the top" and "number on the bottom," when you discuss fractions with your child.*

equivalent fractions Different fractions that represent the same quantity. For example, $\frac{1}{2}$ and $\frac{2}{4}$ are equivalent fractions.

Use with Lesson 7.10.

Do-Anytime Activities

To work with your child on the concepts taught in this unit and in previous units, try these interesting and rewarding activities:

1 Review fraction notation. For example, ask: "In a fraction, what does the number on the bottom (the denominator) tell you?" "What does the number on the top (the numerator) tell you?"

2 Draw a picture of a rectangular cake, a circular pizza, or a similar food (better yet, have the real thing). Discuss ways to cut the food in order to feed various numbers of people so that each person gets an equal portion.

3 Read a recipe and discuss the fractions in it. For example, ask: "How many $\frac{1}{4}$ cups of sugar would we need to get 1 cup of sugar?"

4 Compare two fractions and tell which is larger. For example, ask: "Which would give you more of a pizza: $\frac{1}{8}$ of it, or $\frac{1}{4}$?"

As You Help Your Child with Homework

As your child brings home assignments, you may want to go over the instructions together, clarifying them as necessary. The answers listed below will guide you through this unit's Home Links.

Home Link 8.2

1.

$\frac{1}{2}$ $\frac{1}{4}$ $\frac{1}{2}$ $\frac{3}{4}$

2.

$\frac{1}{4}$ $\frac{1}{2}$ $\frac{3}{4}$ $\frac{1}{2}$

3.

$\frac{1}{2}$ $\frac{1}{3}$ $\frac{1}{6}$ $\frac{5}{6}$

Home Link 8.3

1. 4; 4; 8

Home Link 8.4

1. $\frac{1}{2} = \frac{2}{4}$ 2. $\frac{1}{2} = \frac{4}{8}$ 3. $\frac{1}{4} = \frac{4}{16}$ 4. $\frac{1}{4} = \frac{2}{8}$

5. $\frac{1}{2} = \frac{3}{6}$ 6. $\frac{1}{5} = \frac{4}{20}$

Home Link 8.5

1.   2.

3.

Home Link 8.7

1. $\frac{4}{7}$ 2. 4 tulips   3. $\frac{2}{12}$, or $\frac{1}{6}$ 4. 4 pages

5. $\frac{1}{3}$

Building Skills through Games

In Unit 8, your child will practice multiplication and fraction skills by playing the following games:

Array Bingo

Players roll the dice and find an *Array Bingo* card with the same number of dots. Players then turn that card over. The first player to have a row, column, or diagonal of facedown cards calls "Bingo!" and wins the game.

Equivalent Fractions Game

Players take turns turning over Fraction Cards and try to find matching cards that show equivalent fractions.

Fraction Top-It

Players turn over two Fraction Cards and compare the shaded parts of the cards. The player with the larger fraction keeps both of the cards. The player with more cards at the end wins!

Use with Lesson 7.10.

Equal Parts

Family Note

Help your child collect things that can be easily folded into equal parts. As your child works with fractions, remind him or her that the number under the fraction bar, the *denominator*, gives the total number of equal parts into which the whole is divided. The number over the fraction bar, the *numerator*, tells the number of equal parts that are being considered. Don't expect your child to use these words. They will be learned over time with repeated exposure.

Please return this Home Link to school tomorrow.

Use a straightedge. .

1. Divide the shape into 2 equal parts. Color 1 part.

Part colored = $\dfrac{\boxed{}}{\boxed{}}$ Part not colored = $\dfrac{\boxed{}}{\boxed{}}$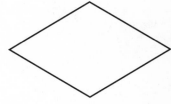

2. Divide the shape into 4 equal parts. Color 3 parts.

Part colored = $\dfrac{\boxed{}}{\boxed{}}$ Part not colored = $\dfrac{\boxed{}}{\boxed{}}$

3. Fold some things into equal parts.

Examples: paper napkin, paper plate, magazine picture

Label each part with a fraction. Show your folded things to someone at home. Talk about what the fractions mean.

Bring the things you folded to school for the Fractions Museum.

I folded a _____ into _____ equal parts.

Each part shows _____.

Fraction Cards

Turn over 2 fractions
cards. Player w/
higher fraction
wins (war)

Fractions of Shapes

Family Note

As you work on this activity with your child, keep in mind that the shapes below the ONE are fractional parts of the ONE. Remind your child that the size of a fractional part of a whole depends on the size of the whole. It may be helpful for your child to separate the ONE into parts that are the size of the fractional part. For example, in Problem 1, your child can divide the square in half diagonally to determine that the triangle is $\frac{1}{2}$ of the square.

Please return this Home Link to school tomorrow.

1. If this is ONE,

then what are these?

Write a fraction for each shape. _____ _____ _____ _____

2. If this is ONE,

then what are these?

Write a fraction for each shape. _____ _____ _____ _____

3. If this is ONE,

then what are these?

Write a fraction for each shape. _____ _____ _____ _____

Family Note

In this lesson, your child learned to use fractions to name part of a collection of objects. For example, your child could identify 2 out of 4 objects as $\frac{2}{4}$ or $\frac{1}{2}$. Show your child how to use pennies to act out Problem 1. Help your child collect household items that can be separated into fractional parts—or any other items that have fractions written on them. Encourage your child to bring these items to school for the class's Fractions Museum.

Please return this Home Link to school tomorrow.

1.

Three people share 12 pennies. Circle each person's share.

How many pennies does each person get? _____ pennies

$\frac{1}{3}$ of 12 pennies = _____ pennies

$\frac{2}{3}$ of 12 pennies = _____ pennies

2. Ask someone at home to help you find more things to bring to school for the Fractions Museum. Here are some ideas:

• Things that can be easily divided into equal parts, such as small collections of dried beans, buttons, or pasta; pieces of string, ribbon, or yarn; pictures of pies, bread, or pizza

• Ads, pictures, milk cartons, or measuring cups that have fractions written on them

• Objects that come in sets, such as a group of buttons or a box of watercolors

Shading Fractional Parts

> **Family Note**
>
> In this lesson, your child learned that a fractional part of a whole can be named in many different ways with *equivalent* fractions. For example, $\frac{2}{4}$, $\frac{4}{8}$, and $\frac{3}{6}$ are names for $\frac{1}{2}$, and $\frac{2}{8}$ and $\frac{4}{16}$ are names for $\frac{1}{4}$. Help your child shade each of the shapes below to show the appropriate fraction. Make sure that your child understands that the fractions are equivalent because they name the same part of the shape.
>
> *Please return this Home Link to school tomorrow.*

1. Shade $\frac{1}{2}$ of the rectangle.

$$\frac{1}{2} = \frac{\square}{4}$$

2. Shade $\frac{1}{2}$ of the rectangle.

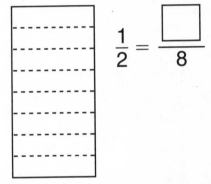

$$\frac{1}{2} = \frac{\square}{8}$$

3. Shade $\frac{1}{4}$ of the square.

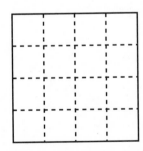

$$\frac{1}{4} = \frac{\square}{16}$$

4. Shade $\frac{1}{4}$ of the square.

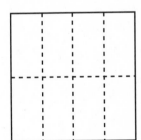

$$\frac{1}{4} = \frac{\square}{8}$$

5. Shade $\frac{1}{2}$ of the rectangle.

$$\frac{1}{2} = \frac{\square}{6}$$

6. Shade $\frac{1}{5}$ of the rectangle.

$$\frac{1}{5} = \frac{\square}{20}$$

Fractions

Family Note

In this lesson, your child has been completing number stories about fractions. Encourage your child to draw pictures or use small objects, such as pennies, to help him or her complete fraction number stories.

Please return this Home Link to school tomorrow.

---

1. 7 children are waiting for the school bus.

4 of them are girls.

What fraction of the children are girls? _____

2. There are 16 tulips in the garden.

$\frac{1}{4}$ of the tulips are red.

How many tulips are red? _____ tulips

3. 12 dogs were in the park.

2 of them were dalmatians.

What fraction of the dogs were dalmatians? _____

4. There are 20 pages in Jamal's book.

He read $\frac{1}{5}$ of the book.

How many pages did he read? _____ pages

5. There are 15 cupcakes.

5 of the cupcakes are chocolate.

What fraction of the cupcakes are chocolate? _____

Family Letter

Unit 9: **Measurement**

In Unit 9, children will explore measurements of various types. Your child will be asked to look for examples of measurements and tools for measuring and to bring them to school to put in our Measures All Around Museum. The examples will help children appreciate the important role that measurement plays in everyday life.

try square
and level

stopwatch

Children will both estimate lengths of distances and actually measure lengths of distances by inch, foot, and yard, as well as centimeter, decimeter, and meter. Children will learn that measurements are always approximations; they will use terms like *close to, between,* and *about* when describing measurements. For more accurate measurements, children will measure to the nearest half-inch and half-centimeter.

In addition to measures of length, children will explore the areas of shapes using square inches and square centimeters. Children will also begin to develop a sense for the size of units of capacity and weight, such as cups and liters and pounds and kilograms.

Everyday Mathematics uses both U.S. customary and metric units of measure. While children make conversions within each system (length, capacity, or weight), they will not yet make conversions from one system to the other.

Please keep this Family Letter for reference as your child works through Unit 9.

Vocabulary

Important terms in Unit 9:

linear measure A measure used to designate length.

weight A measure of the force of gravity on an object or of how heavy something is.

capacity A measure of pourable substances that take the shape of their containers, such as liquids, sand, and rice.

perimeter The distance around a bounded surface. (The peRIMeter measures the "rim.")

area The number of units (usually squares) that can fit into a bounded surface.

area = 4 square units

perimeter = 8 units

Metric System

Units of Length

1 meter (m)	= 10 decimeters (dm)
	= 100 centimeters (cm)
1 decimeter	= 10 centimeters
1 kilometer (km)	= 1,000 meters

Units of Weight

1 kilogram (kg)	= 1,000 grams (g)

Units of Capacity

1 liter (L)	= 1,000 milliliters (mL)
$\frac{1}{2}$ liter	= 500 milliliters

U.S. Customary System

Units of Length

1 yard (yd)	= 3 feet (ft)
	= 36 inches (in.)
1 foot	= 12 inches
1 mile (mi)	= 1,760 yards
	= 5,280 feet

Units of Weight

1 pound (lb)	= 16 ounces (oz)
2,000 pounds	= 1 ton (T)

Units of Capacity

1 cup (c)	= $\frac{1}{2}$ pint (pt)
1 pint	= 2 cups
1 quart (qt)	= 2 pints
1 half-gallon ($\frac{1}{2}$ gal)	= 2 quarts
1 gallon (gal)	= 4 quarts

Use with Lesson 8.8.

Do-Anytime Activities

To work with your child on the concepts taught in this unit and in previous units, try these interesting and rewarding activities:

1 Gather a tape measure, a yardstick, a ruler, a cup, a gallon container, and a scale. Discuss the various things you and your child can measure—for example, the length of a room, how many cups are needed to fill a gallon container, and your child's weight alone and when holding objects, such as books. Record the data and continue to measure and weigh different items periodically.

2 Mark out certain routes on a road map and together figure the distance between two points in both miles and kilometers.

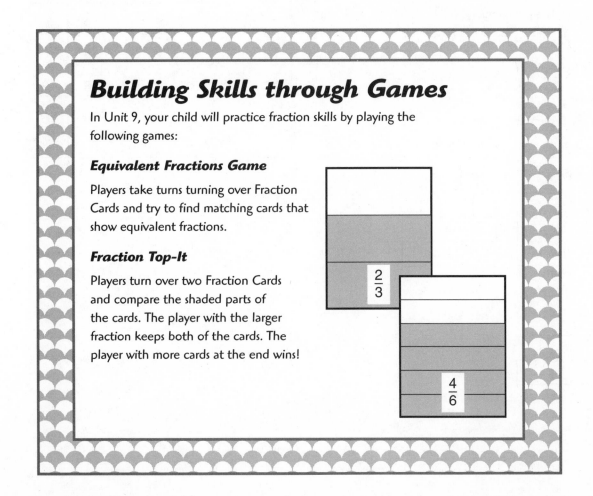

Building Skills through Games

In Unit 9, your child will practice fraction skills by playing the following games:

Equivalent Fractions Game

Players take turns turning over Fraction Cards and try to find matching cards that show equivalent fractions.

Fraction Top-It

Players turn over two Fraction Cards and compare the shaded parts of the cards. The player with the larger fraction keeps both of the cards. The player with more cards at the end wins!

$\frac{2}{3}$

$\frac{4}{6}$

As You Help Your Child with Homework

As your child brings home assignments, you may want to go over the instructions together, clarifying them as necessary. The answers listed below will guide you through this unit's Home Links.

Home Link 9.2

3. 12 inches

4. 3 feet

5. 10 centimeters

6. 100 centimeters

7. 24 inches

8. 9 feet

9. 40 centimeters

10. 700 centimeters

Home Link 9.3

1. $2\frac{1}{2}$ inches

2. 4 inches

3. 3 centimeters

4. 9 centimeters

Home Link 9.4

1. Perimeter: 6 or 7 inches

2. Perimeter: $4\frac{1}{2}$ or 5 inches

3. Answer: 47 feet. Sample number models:

$14 + 14 + 9\frac{1}{2} + 9\frac{1}{2} = 47$ or

$2 \times 14 + 2 \times 9\frac{1}{2} = 47$

Home Link 9.6

1. mile

2. centimeter

3. foot

4. meter

5. inch

6. foot, yard

Home Link 9.7

2.

15 square centimeters

8 square centimeters

3.

Home Link 9.8

1. 9 sq cm

2. 11 sq cm

3. 10 sq cm

4. I: 20 cm

U: 24 cm

J: 22 cm

Home Link 9.9

Rule	
1 gal = 4 qt	
gal	**qt**
2	8
4	16
6	24
10	40

Rule	
1 pt = 2 c	
pt	**c**
2	4
3	6
5	10
7	14

Rule	
1 qt = 2 pt	
qt	**pt**
2	4
4	8
6	12
8	16

Using Measurement

Family Note

In class today, your child measured distances by using a yardstick. Talk with your child about measurements that you use at your job, around the house, in sports, or in other activities. If you don't have measuring tools to show your child, you might find pictures of measuring tools in a catalog, magazine, or book. Discuss with your child how these tools are used.

Please return this Home Link to school tomorrow.

1. Talk with people at home about how they use measurements at home, at their jobs, or in other activities.

2. Ask people at home to show you the tools they use for measuring. Write the names of some of these tools. Be ready to talk about your list in class.

_____   _____

_____   _____

_____   _____

_____   _____

3. Look for measures in pictures in newspapers or magazines. For example, an ad might name the height of a bookcase or tell how much a container holds. Ask an adult if you may bring the pictures to school for our Measures All Around Museum. Circle the measures.

4. Bring one or two small boxes shaped like rectangular prisms to school. The boxes should be small enough to fit on a sheet of paper.

Linear Measurements

Family Note

Today your child reviewed how to use a ruler to measure objects and distances in inches and feet and in centimeters and decimeters. Your child's class also began making a Table of Equivalencies for both the U.S. customary and the metric systems. Ask your child to show you how to measure some of the objects or distances that he or she selects to complete the tables below.

Please return this Home Link to school tomorrow.

1. Cut out the 6-inch ruler on the next page. Measure two objects or distances. Measure to the nearest foot. Then measure again to the nearest inch. Some things you might measure are the width of the refrigerator door, the length of the bathtub, or the height of a light switch from the floor.

Object *or* Distance	Nearest Foot	Nearest Inch
	about ____ ft	about ____ in.
	about ____ ft	about ____ in.

2. Cut out the 10-inch centimeter ruler on the next page. Measure the same objects or distances. Measure to the nearest decimeter. Then measure again to the nearest centimeter.

Object *or* Distance	Nearest Decimeter	Nearest Centimeter
	about ____ dm	about ____ cm
	about ____ dm	about ____ cm

Linear Measurements (cont.)

Complete each sentence.

3. One foot is equal to _____ inches.

4. One yard is equal to _____ feet.

5. One decimeter is equal to _____ centimeters.

6. One meter is equal to _____ centimeters.

7. Two feet are equal to _____ inches.

8. Three yards are equal to _____ feet.

9. Four decimeters are equal to _____ centimeters.

10. Seven meters are equal to _____ centimeters.

Use with Lesson 9.2.

Measuring Lengths

Family Note

Today your child measured life-size pictures of objects to the nearest half-inch and half-centimeter. Take turns with your child measuring objects to the nearest half-inch and half-centimeter. Check to see if your measurements are the same.

Please return this Home Link to school tomorrow.

Cut out the 6-inch ruler on the next page. Measure each line segment to the nearest half-inch. Write the measurement in the blank to the right of each segment.

1. _____ _____ inches

2. _____ _____ inches

Cut out the 15-centimeter ruler on the next page. Measure each line segment to the nearest half-centimeter. Write the measurement in the blank to the right of each segment.

3. _____ _____ centimeters

4. _____ _____ centimeters

Measure some things in your home to the nearest half-inch or half-centimeter. List the things and their measurements below.

Thing	**Measurement**
5. _____	_____
6. _____	_____
7. _____	_____
8. _____	_____

Measuring Lengths (cont.)

9. Draw pictures of two things you measured. Mark the parts you measured. Record the measurements under the pictures.

Use with Lesson 9.3.

Travel Interview

Family Note

Our class is studying measurement of longer distances. If the traveler your child talks to had experiences with the metric system in another country, have your child include this information to share with the class.

Please return this Home Link to school tomorrow.

Ask someone at home to tell you about the longest trip he or she ever took. Write about the trip. Here are some questions you might want to ask that person:

- When did you take the trip?

- Where did you go?

- What interesting or unusual things did you see or do?

- How did you travel? By car? By plane? By train?

- How long did the trip take?

- How far did you travel?

_____

_____

_____

_____

_____

_____

Units of Measure

Family Note

Today in class, your child identified appropriate measuring tools and units of measure for various items. All of the items below may be measured with any of the given units. There are, however, some units that are best suited for measuring short distances and some units that are best suited for measuring longer distances. Help your child decide which unit is best for each situation.

Please return this Home Link to school tomorrow.

Circle the unit that you would use to measure each item.

1. distance from Orlando, Florida, to Boston, Massachusetts

inch

foot

mile

2. length of a paper clip

centimeter

meter

kilometer

3. height of your teacher

yard

foot

mile

4. perimeter of your bedroom

centimeter

meter

kilometer

5. width of a deck of cards

inch

foot

yard

6. length of a bus

inch

foot

yard

Capacity and Area

Family Note

Today your child explored the ideas of *capacity* and *area*. Before your child is exposed to formal work with these measures (such as equivalent units of capacity or formulas for finding area), it is important that he or she have an informal understanding of these measures.

In Problem 1, help your child see that although the glasses may have different dimensions, they can still hold about the same amount of water. In Problems 2 and 3, the number of squares that your child counts is the area in square centimeters.

Please return this Home Link to school tomorrow.

1. Find two different glasses at home that you think hold about the same amount of water. Test your prediction by pouring water from one glass into the other. Do they hold about the same amount of water? Does one glass hold more than the other? Explain to someone at home how you know.

2. Count squares to find the area of each figure.

_____ square centimeters   _____ square centimeters

3. Circle the shape that has the larger area.

Capacity

Family Note

Today children discussed units of capacity. Capacity is a measure of how much liquid (or other pourable substance, such as sand or rice) a container can hold. Your child recorded equivalent U.S. customary units of capacity (cup, pint, quart, half-gallon, gallon) and equivalent metric units of capacity (milliliter, liter). Please help your child pick out a recipe and identify the units of capacity in the list of ingredients.

Please return this Home Link to school tomorrow.

Ask someone at home to help you find a recipe that uses units of capacity. Copy those ingredients and the amounts called for by the recipe. Bring your list to school.

Example: $\frac{3}{4}$ *cup of milk*

_____

_____

"What's My Rule?"

Rule	
1 gal = 4 qt	

gal	qt
2	
	16
6	
10	

Rule	
1 pt = 2 c	

pt	c
2	
3	
	10
	14

Rule	
1 qt = 2 pt	

qt	pt
2	
4	
	12
8	

Weight

Family Note

In today's lesson, children discussed U.S. customary units of weight (pounds, ounces) and metric units of weight (grams, kilograms). Your child weighed different objects using a variety of scales. Help your child weigh items using scales in your home, or find items with weights written on them.

Please this return this Home Link to school tomorrow.

Find out what kinds of scales you have at home—for example, a bath scale, a letter scale, or a package scale. Weigh a variety of things on the scales, such as a person, a letter, or a book. Record your results below.

If you don't have any scales, look for cans and packages of food with weights written on them. Record those weights below. Remember that ounces (oz) measure weight and that fluid ounces (fl oz) measure capacity.

Object	**Weight** (include unit)
_____	_____
_____	_____
_____	_____
_____	_____
_____	_____
_____	_____

Family Letter

Unit 10: Decimals and Place Value

In this unit, children will review money concepts, such as names of coins and bills, money exchanges, and equivalent amounts. They will pretend to pay for items and to make change.

The unit also focuses on extending work with fractions and money by using decimal notation. Children will use calculators for money problems and estimation.

Later in this unit, children will work with place-value notation for 5–digit numbers. Here, as previously, the focus remains on strategies that help children automatically think of any digit in a numeral in terms of its value as determined by its place. For example, children will learn that in a number like 7,843, the 8 stands for 800, not 8, and the 4 for 40, not 4.

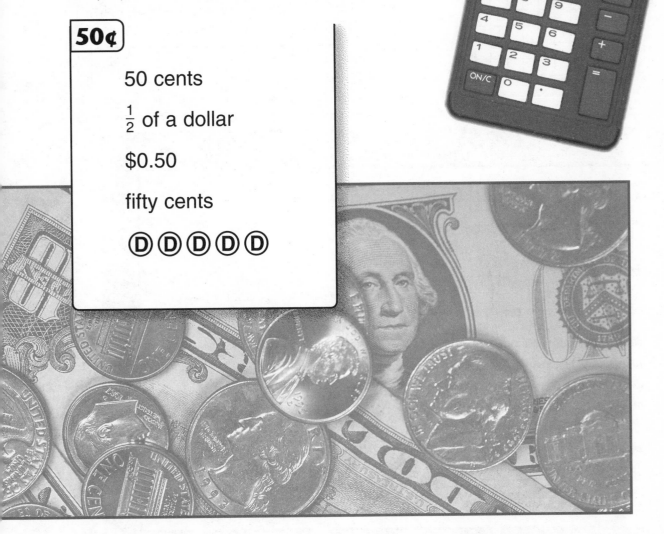

50¢

50 cents

$\frac{1}{2}$ of a dollar

$0.50

fifty cents

Ⓓ Ⓓ Ⓓ Ⓓ Ⓓ

Please keep this Family Letter for reference as your child works through Unit 10.

Vocabulary

Important terms in Unit 10:

decimal point The period that separates the whole number from the fraction in decimal notation. In money amounts, it separates the dollars from the fractions of a dollar (the cents).

flat A base-10 block that represents 100.

long A base-10 block that represents 10.

cube A base-10 block that represents 1.

place value The relative worth of each digit in a number, as determined by the digit's position. Each place has a value ten times that of the place to its right and one-tenth that of the place to its left. The chart below illustrates the place value of each digit in 7,843.

7	8	4	3
↑	↑	↑	↑
thousands	hundreds	tens	ones

Building Skills through Games

In Unit 10, your child will build his or her understanding of fractions and money by playing the following games:

Fraction Top-It

Players turn over two fraction cards and compare the shaded parts of the cards. The player with the larger fraction keeps both of the cards. The player with more cards at the end wins!

Money Exchange Game

Players roll a die and put that number of $1 bills on their Place-Value Mats. Whenever possible, they exchange ten $1 bills for one $10 bill. The first player to make an exchange for one $100 bill wins!

Pick-a-Coin

Players create coin collections based on rolls of a die. Players try to get the largest possible values for their collections.

Use with Lesson 9.11.

Do-Anytime Activities

To work with your child on the concepts taught in this unit and in previous units, try these interesting and rewarding activities:

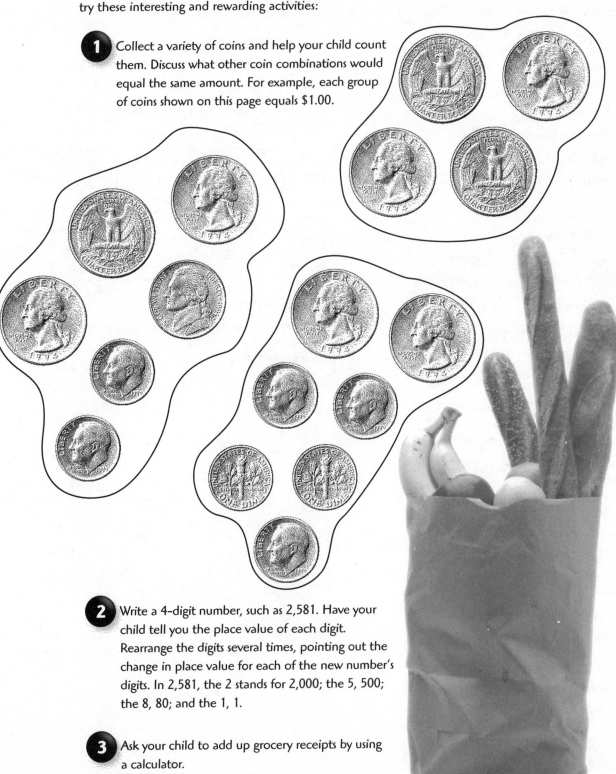

1 Collect a variety of coins and help your child count them. Discuss what other coin combinations would equal the same amount. For example, each group of coins shown on this page equals $1.00.

2 Write a 4-digit number, such as 2,581. Have your child tell you the place value of each digit. Rearrange the digits several times, pointing out the change in place value for each of the new number's digits. In 2,581, the 2 stands for 2,000; the 5, 500; the 8, 80; and the 1, 1.

3 Ask your child to add up grocery receipts by using a calculator.

As You Help Your Child with Homework

As your child brings home assignments, you may want to go over the instructions together, clarifying them as necessary. The answers listed below will guide you through this unit's Home Links.

Home Link 10.1

1. 10 pennies = 10¢, or $0.10

10 nickels = 50¢, or $0.50

10 dimes = $1.00

10 quarters = $2.50

10 half-dollars = $5.00

Total = $9.10

Home Link 10.2

1. $3.57   **2.** $3.55   **3.** $0.52   **4.** $0.08

5. Sample answers: $1 $1 Q Q D P P P P or
$1 Q Q Q Q D D D D N N N N P P P

Home Link 10.3

1. $0.06; $0.50; $1.30; $1.50; $3.36

Home Link 10.4

1. 1.09; 2.5; 0.98; 3.18; 0.06

Home Link 10.5

1. $0.70   **2.** $2.60   **3.** $1.00

4. $1.30   **5.** $4.00   **6.** $1.20

7. $2.30   **8.** $1.30 + $0.50 = $1.80

9. $0.80 + $0.40 = $1.20

10. $0.70 + $0.90 = $1.60

11. $1.40 + $0.80 = $2.20

Home Link 10.7

1. 17 square cm   **2.** 17 sq cm

3. 23 cm²   **4.** 10 square cm

5. 9 sq cm   **6.** 9 cm²

Home Link 10.8

1. ④6 2   **2.** 1,③26   **3.** 5,⓪06

4. ⑧69   **5.** 2,③04   **6.** 4,⑤67

9. 1,183   **10.** 1,204   **11.** 1,050

Home Link 10.9

1. 0; 100; 200; 300; 400; 500; 600; 700; 800; 900; 1,000

2. 0; 1,000; 2,000; 3,000; 4,000; 5,000; 6,000; 7,000; 8,000; 9,000; 10,000

3.

Number	10 More	100 More	1,000 More
32	42	132	1,032
146	156	246	1,146
309	319	409	1,309
1,468	1,478	1,568	2,468
10,037	10,047	10,137	11,037

Home Link 10.10

3. 72,469   **4.** 72,569; 75,469; 72,369; 69,469

Home Link 10.11

1. 9   **2.** 15   **3.** 13   **4.** 6

5. 13 − (9 + 2) = 2

6. (28 − 8) − 4 = 16

7. (150 − 70) − 40 = 40

8. 800 − (200 + 300) = 300

9. 15

25 = (15 + 5)

(25 − 15) + 5

(17 − 9) + 7

17 − (9 + 7)

(3 + 6) + 6

3 + (6 + 6)

10. 100

(50 + 150) − 100

50 + (150 − 100)

400 = (300 − 200)

(400 − 300) + 200

Coin Combinations

Family Note

In today's lesson, your child practiced writing amounts of money. For example, in Problem 1, 10 pennies can be written as 10¢ or $0.10. Your child also showed different groups of coins that have the same monetary value. For example, your child could show 62¢ with 2 quarters, 1 dime, and 2 pennies; or 4 dimes, 4 nickels, and 2 pennies. For Problem 2, help your child find items in newspaper or magazine ads and think of different combinations of coins and bills to pay for the items.

Please return this Home Link to school tomorrow.

1. Pretend that you have 10 of each kind of coin.
How much is that in all?

10 pennies   = _____

10 nickels   = _____

10 dimes   = _____

10 quarters   = _____

10 half-dollars = _____

Total   = _____

2. Find two ads in a newspaper or magazine for items that cost less than $3.00 each.

• Ask for permission to cut out the ads.

• Cut them out and glue them onto the back of this page.

• Draw coins to show the cost of each item.

(If you can't find ads, draw pictures of items and prices on the back of this page.)

Name   Date   Time

How Much?

Family Note

In today's lesson, your child practiced reading and writing money amounts using dollars and cents. Ask your child to read each amount aloud. Remind your child that the digits before the decimal point stand for whole dollars; the digits after the decimal point stand for cents. When reading amounts, such as "3 dollars and fifty-seven cents," the word "and" is used to denote the decimal point.

Please return this Home Link to school tomorrow.

How much money? Write your answer in dollars-and-cents notation.

1. $1 $1 $1 Q Q N P P $___.___

2. $1 $1 Q Q Q Q D D D N N N N N $___.___

3. Q D D P P P P P P P $___.___

4. N P P P $___.___

5. Use $1 , Q, D, N, and P to draw $2.64 in two different ways.

Calculators and Money

Family Note

In today's lesson, your child used a calculator to solve problems with money. In Problem 2, your child will ask you or another adult to compare the cost of an item when you were a child to its current cost. There are two ways to make this type of comparison. You might describe a *difference comparison*. For example: "A bicycle costs about $90.00 more now than it did then." You might also use a *ratio comparison*. For example, "A bicycle costs about 4 times as much now as it did then." You do not need to share the terms "difference comparison" and "ratio comparison" with your child, but it is important that your child be exposed to both types of comparisons.

Please return this Home Link to school tomorrow.

1. Enter the following amounts into your calculator.
   What does your calculator show?

   Enter   **Calculator Shows**

   $1.09   _____

   $2.50   _____

   98¢   _____

   $3.18   _____

   6¢   _____

2. Ask an adult to think about an item that he or she remembers from when he or she was a child. Ask the adult to compare how much the item cost then and now. Make a record below of what you find out.

   _____

   _____

   _____

Estimation to the Nearest 10¢

Family Note

In today's lesson, your child estimated sums by first finding the nearest ten cents for each amount of money being added and then adding the amounts for the nearest ten cents together. For Problems 1–7, ask your child how she or he arrived at each answer. If needed, use coins to show which amount is actually closer. For Problems 8–11, help your child find the totals by thinking of a problem like $1.20 + $0.60 as 12 + 6 or as 120 cents + 60 cents.

Please return this Home Link to school tomorrow.

Write the correct answer to each question.
Talk with someone at home about your answers.

1. Is $0.69 closer to $0.60 or $0.70? _____

2. Is $2.59 closer to $2.50 or $2.60? _____

3. Is $0.99 closer to $0.90 or $1.00? _____

4. Is $1.31 closer to $1.30 or $1.40? _____

5. Is $3.99 closer to $3.90 or $4.00? _____

6. Is $1.17 closer to $1.10 or $1.20? _____

7. Is $2.34 closer to $2.30 or $2.40? _____

Fill in the blanks and estimate the total cost in each problem.

Example

$1.19 + $0.59 is about ___*$1.20*___ + ___*$0.60*___ = ___*$1.80*___ .

8. $1.29 + $0.48 is about _____ + _____ = _____ .

9. $0.79 + $0.39 is about _____ + _____ = _____ .

10. $0.69 + $0.89 is about _____ + _____ = _____ .

11. $1.41 + $0.77 is about _____ + _____ = _____ .

Area

Family Note

In today's lesson, your child found the area of shapes by counting square centimeters. As you observe your child finding the areas below, check that he or she is counting squares that are more than $\frac{1}{2}$ shaded as 1 square centimeter and not counting squares that are less than $\frac{1}{2}$ shaded. For Problem 6, see if your child has a suggestion for what to do if exactly $\frac{1}{2}$ of a square is shaded. Remind your child that area is reported in square units. Other ways to write square centimeters are **sq cm** and **cm²**.

Please return this Home Link to school tomorrow.

Count squares to find the area of each shaded figure.

1.

_____ square cm

2.

_____ sq cm

3.

_____ cm²

4.

_____ square cm

5.

_____ sq cm

6.

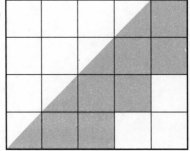

_____ cm²

Place Value

Family Note

In this lesson, your child has been studying place value, or the value of digits in numbers. Listen as your child reads the numbers in Problems 1–6. You might ask your child to pick a few of the numbers and tell you the place value of each of the digits. For example, in 462, the value of 4 is 400, the value of 6 is 60, and the value of 2 is 2.

Please return this Home Link to school tomorrow.

In each number: • Circle the digit in the hundreds place.

                     • Underline the digit in the thousands place.

Example: 9 , ③ 4 2

1. 4 6 2

2. 1 , 3 2 6

3. 5 , 0 0 6

4. 8 6 9

5. 2 , 3 0 4

6. 4 , 5 6 7

7. Read the numbers in Problems 1–6 to someone at home.

Write the numbers represented by the base-10 blocks.

8. = _____247_____

9. = _____

10. = _____

11. = _____

Counting by 10s, 100s, and 1,000s

Family Note

In this lesson, your child used place value to count by 10s, 100s, and 1,000s. For Problems 1 and 2, listen carefully to find out if your child counts quickly and accurately. Help your child complete the table in Problem 3. If necessary, have your child use a calculator to find the answers. Ask your child to describe any patterns he or she sees in the completed table.

Please return this Home Link to school tomorrow.

1. Show someone at home how to count by 100s from 0 to 1,000. Record your counts.

_____

_____

2. Now count by 1,000s from 0 to 10,000. Record your counts.

_____

_____

3. Complete the table.

Number	10 More	100 More	1,000 More
32	42	132	1,032
146			
309			
1,468			
10,037			

4-Digit and 5-Digit Numbers

Family Note

In this lesson, your child read and displayed 4- and 5-digit numbers. Listen to your child read numbers to you. Remind your child not to say "and" when reading numbers, such as the ones below. (In reading numbers, "and" indicates a decimal point. For example, 7.9 is read as "seven and nine tenths.") However, don't go out of your way to correct your child if he or she inserts "and" occasionally. For Problem 2, write some 4- and 5-digit numbers as your child is writing numbers. Exchange your sets of numbers and read each other's numbers aloud.

Please return this Home Link to school tomorrow.

1. Read these numbers to someone at home.

   3,426; 6,001; 9,864; 13,400; 29,368; 99,999

2. Write other 4- and 5-digit numbers. Read your numbers to someone at home.

_____

3. Write a number that has:

   4 in the hundreds place.

   6 in the tens place.

   2 in the thousands place.

   7 in the ten-thousands place.

   9 in the ones place.

   ____ ____ , ____ ____ ____

4. Use the number in Problem 3. What number is

   100 more? _____

   3,000 more? _____

   100 less? _____

   3,000 less? _____

Grouping with Parentheses

Home Link
10.11

Family Note

In this lesson, your child has solved problems and puzzles involving parentheses. For Problems 1–4, 9, and 10, remind your child that the calculations inside of the parentheses need to be done first. In Problem 1, for example, your child should first find $7 - 2$ and then add that answer (5) to 4. For Problems 5–8, observe as your child adds parentheses. Ask your child to explain what to do first in order to obtain the number on the right side of the equals sign.

Please return this Home Link to school tomorrow.

Solve problems containing parentheses.

1. $4 + (7 - 2) =$ _____

2. $(9 + 21) - 15 =$ _____

3. $6 + (12 - 5) =$ _____

4. $(15 + 5) - 14 =$ _____

Put in parentheses to solve the puzzles.

5. $13 - 9 + 2 = 2$

6. $28 - 8 - 4 = 16$

7. $150 - 70 - 40 = 40$

8. $800 - 200 + 300 = 300$

Cross out the names that don't belong in the name-collection boxes.

9.

15
$25 - (15 + 5)$
$(25 - 15) + 5$
$(17 - 9) + 7$
$17 - (9 + 7)$
$(3 + 6) + 6$
$3 + (6 + 6)$

10.

100
$(50 + 150) - 100$
$50 + (150 - 100)$
$400 - (300 - 200)$
$(400 - 300) + 200$

Family Letter

Unit 11:
Whole-Number Operations Revisited

In the beginning of Unit 11, children will solve addition and subtraction stories with dollars and cents. Children will use estimation to examine their answers and determine whether the answers make sense.

Children will also review the uses of multiplication and division and begin to develop multiplication and division fact power, or the ability to automatically recall the basic multiplication and division facts.

Children will work with shortcuts, which will help them extend known facts to related facts. For example, the **turn-around rule for multiplication** shows that the order of the numbers being multiplied (the factors) does not affect the product; 3×4 is the same as 4×3. Children will also learn what it means to multiply a number by 0 and by 1. Patterns in a Facts Table and in fact families will also help children explore ways of learning multiplication and division facts.

×, ÷	1	2	3	4	5	6	7	8	9	10
1	1	2	3	4	5	6	7	8	9	10
2	2	4	6	8	10	12	14	16	18	20
3	3	6	9	12	15	18	21	24	27	30
4	4	8	12	16	20	24	28	32	36	40
5	5	10	15	20	25	30	35	40	45	50
6	6	12	18	24	30	36	42	48	54	60
7	7	14	21	28	35	42	49	56	63	70
8	8	16	24	32	40	48	56	64	72	80
9	9	18	27	36	45	54	63	72	81	90
10	10	20	30	40	50	60	70	80	90	100

Multiplication/Division Facts Table

Finally, children will apply and extend their knowledge as they analyze and compare precipitation data obtained from a map.

Please keep this Family Letter for reference as your child works through Unit 11.

Vocabulary

Important terms in Unit 11:

multiplication diagram A diagram used to represent numbers in which several equal groups are being considered together. The diagram has three parts: a number of groups, a number in each group, and a total number.

Multiplication Diagram

rows	_____ per row	_____ in all

Number model: _____ × _____ = _____

---

factor One of the numbers being multiplied in a multiplication number model.

$$\text{factors} \qquad \text{product}$$
$$4 \quad \times \quad 5 \quad = \quad 20$$

product The result of doing multiplication.

quotient The whole-number result when one number is divided by another number; the number of equal shares.

remainder The amount left over (if any) when a number is divided into equal shares.

$$\text{quotient} \qquad \text{remainder}$$
$$14 \div 5 \quad \rightarrow \quad 2 \qquad\qquad R4$$

fact power The ability to automatically recall basic multiplication and division facts.

turn-around rule for multiplication The order of numbers being multiplied does not affect the outcome. For example, $3 \times 4 = 12$ and $4 \times 3 = 12$.

fact family A collection of related addition and subtraction facts, or multiplication and division facts, made from the same numbers. For the numbers 3, 5, and 15, for example, the fact family consists of $3 \times 5 = 15$, $5 \times 3 = 15$, $15 \div 3 = 5$, and $15 \div 5 = 3$.

middle value The number in the middle when a set of data is organized in sequential order; also called the median. For example, in the set of data below, 35 is the middle value.

$$32 \quad 32 \quad 34 \quad 35 \quad 35 \quad 37 \quad 38$$

range The difference between the greatest and least numbers in a set of data. For example, in the set of data above, 6 is the range ($38 - 32 = 6$).

Use with Lesson 10.12.

Do-Anytime Activities

To work with your child on the concepts taught in this unit and in previous units, try these interesting and rewarding activities:

1 Review common multiplication shortcuts. Ask, for example: *What happens when you multiply a number by 1? By 0? By 10?* Use pennies to show that 2 × 3 pennies is the same as 3 × 2 pennies.

2 At a restaurant or while grocery shopping, work together to estimate the bill.

3 Take turns making up multiplication and division number stories to solve.

Building Skills through Games

In Unit 11, your child will practice multiplication skills and mental arithmetic by playing the following games:

Beat the Calculator

A "Calculator" (a player who uses a calculator to solve the problem) and a "Brain" (a player who solves the problem without a calculator) race to see who will be first to solve multiplication problems.

Hit the Target

Players choose a 2-digit multiple of ten as a "target number." One player enters a "starting number" into a calculator and tries to change the starting number to the target number by adding a number to it on the calculator. Children practice finding differences between 2-digit numbers and higher multiples of tens.

Use with Lesson 10.12.

As You Help Your Child with Homework

As your child brings home assignments, you may want to go over the instructions together, clarifying them as necessary. The answers listed below will guide you through this unit's Home Links.

Home Link 11.1

1. $2.22   **2.** $4.06   **3.** $3.34   **4.** $1.64

Home Link 11.2

1. glue stick; $0.14   **2.** glitter; $0.58

3. coloring pencils; $1.12   **4.** coloring pencils; $1.84

5. $0.11   **6.** $2.41

Home Link 11.3

1. 18 tennis balls; $6 \times 3 = 18$

2. 32 buns; $4 \times 8 = 32$

Home Link 11.4

1. 6 packages; $18 \div 3 \rightarrow 6$ R0

2. 6 cards; $25 \div 4 \rightarrow 6$ R1

Home Link 11.5

1. 12   **2.** 12   **3.** 10

4. 9

5. 14

6. 12

7. 2 nickels = 10 cents; $2 \times 5 = 10$

6 nickels = 30 cents; $6 \times 5 = 30$

8. 4 dimes = 40 cents; $4 \times 10 = 40$

7 dimes = 70 cents; $7 \times 10 = 70$

9. double 6 = 12; $2 \times 6 = 12$

double 9 = 18; $2 \times 9 = 18$

Home Link 11.6

2. a. 99   **b.** 502   **c.** 0   **d.** 0

Home Link 11.8

1. $5 \times 7 = 35$ **2.** $3 \times 6 = 18$

$7 \times 5 = 35$ $6 \times 3 = 18$

$35 \div 5 = 7$ $18 \div 3 = 6$

$35 \div 7 = 5$ $18 \div 6 = 3$

3. $4 \times 6 = 24$ **4.** $5 \times 6 = 30$

$6 \times 4 = 24$ $6 \times 5 = 30$

$24 \div 4 = 6$ $30 \div 5 = 6$

$24 \div 6 = 4$ $30 \div 6 = 5$

Home Link 11.9

1. Dave; 40 years   **2.** Lily; 8 years

3. 32 years   **4.** 12 years

5. Lily   **6.** Diane

7. Jillian   **8.** Dave

246

Buying Art Supplies

**Family
Note**

In today's lesson, your child solved number stories involving money amounts. Ask your child to explain to you how he or she solved each of the addition problems below. Challenge your child to find the total cost of 3 or 4 items. Encourage your child to use estimation before solving each problem. Ask such questions as: *Is the total cost of the crayons and glitter more or less than $3.00?* (less)

Please return this Home Link to school tomorrow.

| **Crayons** | **Glitter** | **Coloring Pencils** | **Glue Stick** |
| $0.75 | $1.47 | $2.59 | $0.89 |

Find the total cost of each pair of items.

1. crayons and glitter Total cost: _____	**2.** glitter and coloring pencils Total cost: _____
3. crayons and coloring pencils Total cost: _____	**4.** glue stick and crayons Total cost: _____

Comparing Costs

Family Note

In today's lesson, your child solved subtraction number stories involving money amounts. Ask your child to explain how he or she solved each of the subtraction problems below. Encourage your child to use estimation before solving each problem. Ask such questions as: *Is the difference in cost between the crayons and glitter more or less than $1.00?* (less)

Please return this Home Link to school tomorrow.

$0.75

Crayons

$1.47

Glitter

$2.59

Coloring Pencils

$0.89

Glue Stick

In Problems 1–4, circle the item that costs more.
Then find how much more.

1. glue stick or crayons

How much more? _____

2. glue stick or glitter

How much more? _____

3. glitter or coloring pencils

How much more? _____

4. coloring pencils or crayons

How much more? _____

5. Jenna bought a glue stick. She paid with a $1 bill. How much change should she get?

_____

6. Denisha bought a set of coloring pencils. She paid with a $5 bill. How much change should she get?

_____

Multiplication Number Stories

Family Note

In today's lesson, your child solved multiplication number stories in which he or she found the total number of things in several equal groups. Observe the strategies your child uses to solve the problems below. The "multiplication diagram" is a device used to keep track of the information in a problem.

To solve Problem 1, your child would identify the known information by writing a 6 under *cans* and a 3 under *tennis balls per can*. To identify the unknown information, your child would write a ? under *tennis balls in all*.

Please return this Home Link to school tomorrow.

Show someone at home how to solve these multiplication stories.
Fill in each multiplication diagram.
Use counters or draw pictures or arrays to help you.

1. The store has 6 cans of tennis balls.
   There are 3 balls in each can.
   How many tennis balls are there in all?

<u>cans</u>	tennis balls per <u>can</u>	tennis balls in all

Answer: _____ tennis balls

Number model: _____ × _____ = _____

Multiplication Stories (cont.)

2. Hamburger buns come in packages of 8.
You buy 4 packages.
How many buns are there in all?

packages	buns per package	buns in all

Answer: _____ buns

Number model: _____ × _____ = _____

3. Make up and solve a multiplication number story below.

_____

_____

_____

_____	_____ per _____	_____ in all

Answer: _____

Number model: _____ × _____ = _____

Use with Lesson 11.3.

Division Number Stories

Family Note

Today your child solved division number stories about equal sharing and equal groups. The diagram used for multiplication can also be used for division number stories to identify known and unknown information. Your child will write a number model for each problem below. A number model is the symbolic representation of a number story. For example, in Problem 1, the number model is $18 \div 3 \rightarrow 6$ R0. This model is read as *18 divided by 6 gives 3, remainder 0*. An arrow is used instead of an equals (=) sign because the result of a division problem can be two whole numbers: the quotient and remainder.

Please return this Home Link to school tomorrow.

Show someone at home how to solve these division stories.
Use counters or draw pictures or diagrams to help you.

1. Our group needs 18 pens. There are 3 pens in each package. How many packages must we buy?

packages	pens per package	pens in all

Answer: _____ packages

Number model: _____ ÷ _____ → _____ R _____

2. Four children are playing a game with 25 cards. How many cards can the dealer give each player?

children	cards per child	cards in all

Answer: _____ cards

Number model: _____ ÷ _____ → _____ R _____

3. Make up and solve a division story on the back of this sheet.

Multiplication Facts

Family Note

In this lesson, your child has been learning multiplication facts and has used arrays to represent those facts. The first factor in a multiplication fact tells the number of rows in the array, and the second factor tells the number of columns in the array. In Problem 1, for example, an array with 2 rows of 6 dots is used for the multiplication fact $2 \times 6 = 12$.

Please return this Home Link to school tomorrow.

Show someone at home how you can use arrays to find products. Use •s.

1. $2 \times 6 =$ _____ • • • • • • • • • • • •	**2.** $6 \times 2 =$ _____	**3.** $1 \times 10 =$ _____
4. $1 \times 9 =$ _____	**5.** $2 \times 7 =$ _____	**6.** $3 \times 4 =$ _____

7. 2 nickels = _____ cents $2 \times 5 =$ _____

  6 nickels = _____ cents $6 \times 5 =$ _____

8. 4 dimes = _____ cents $4 \times 10 =$ _____

  7 dimes = _____ cents $7 \times 10 =$ _____

9. double 6 = _____ $2 \times 6 =$ _____

  double 9 = _____ $2 \times 9 =$ _____

Multiplication Facts

Family Note

In today's lesson, your child practiced multiplication facts by using a table and discussed patterns in multiplication facts. For example, any number multiplied by 1 is that number; any number multiplied by 0 is 0; and if the order of the factors in a multiplication fact is reversed, the product remains the same.

Observe the strategies your child uses to find the answers below. By the end of second grade, your child should be proficient with 0s and 1s facts and developing proficiency with the 2s, 5s, and 10s facts.

Please return this Home Link to school tomorrow.

1. Show someone at home what you know about multiplication facts. You can use arrays or pictures to help solve the problems.

0 × 9 = ____	8 × 0 = ____	4 × 0 = ____	0 × 7 = ____
1 × 3 = ____	3 × 1 = ____	1 × 8 = ____	10 × 1 = ____
2 × 8 = ____	3 × 2 = ____	2 × 7 = ____	4 × 2 = ____
5 × 3 = ____	2 × 5 = ____	6 × 5 = ____	5 × 8 = ____
10 × 4 = ____	3 × 10 = ____	9 × 10 = ____	10 × 6 = ____

2. Explain to someone at home why it is easy to solve the following multiplication problems.

a.   99
    × 1
————

b.   502
    × 1
————

c.   37
    × 0
————

d.   15,461
    ×   0
————

3. Make up and solve some multiplication problems of your own on the back of this page.

×, ÷ Fact Triangles

Family Note

Fact Triangles are tools for building mental arithmetic skills. You might think of them as the *Everyday Mathematics* version of the flash cards that you may remember from grade school. Fact Triangles, however, are more effective for helping children memorize facts because they emphasize fact families.

A **fact family** is a collection of related facts made from the same three numbers. For the numbers 4, 6, and 24, the multiplication/division fact family consists of $4 \times 6 = 24$, $6 \times 4 = 24$, $24 \div 6 = 4$, and $24 \div 4 = 6$.

Please help your child cut out the Fact Triangles attached to this letter.

To use Fact Triangles to practice multiplication with your child, cover the number next to the dot with your thumb. The number you have covered is the product.

Your child uses the numbers that are showing to tell you one or two multiplication facts: $3 \times 5 = 15$ or $5 \times 3 = 15$.

Multiplication

To practice division, use your thumb to cover a number without a dot.

Your child uses the numbers that are showing to tell you the division fact $15 \div 5 = 3$.

Now cover the other number without a dot. Your child now tells you the other division fact $15 \div 3 = 5$.

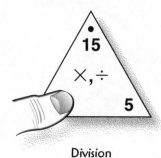

Division

If your child misses a fact, flash the other two fact problems on the card and then return to the fact that was missed.

Example: Sue can't answer $15 \div 3$. Flash 3×5, then $15 \div 5$, and finally $15 \div 3$ a second time.

Make this activity brief and fun. Spend about 10 minutes each night for the next few weeks, or until your child masters all of the facts. The work you do at home will support the work your child is doing at school.

Division

×, ÷ Fact Triangles (cont.)

Cut out the Fact Triangles. Show someone at home how you can use them to practice multiplication and division facts.

Fact Families

Family Note

Today your child continued to practice multiplication and division facts by playing a game called *Beat the Calculator* and by using Fact Triangles. Observe as your child writes the fact family for each Fact Triangle below. Use the Fact Triangles that your child brought home yesterday. Spend about 10 minutes practicing facts with your child. Make the activity brief and fun. The work you do at home will support the work your child is doing at school.

Please return this Home Link to school tomorrow.

Write the fact family for each Fact Triangle.

1.

$$\underline{5} \times \underline{7} = \underline{35}$$

$$\underline{} \times \underline{} = \underline{}$$

$$\underline{35} \div \underline{5} = \underline{7}$$

$$\underline{} \div \underline{} = \underline{}$$

2.

$$\underline{} \times \underline{} = \underline{}$$

$$\underline{} \times \underline{} = \underline{}$$

$$\underline{} \div \underline{} = \underline{}$$

$$\underline{} \div \underline{} = \underline{}$$

3.

$$\underline{} \times \underline{} = \underline{}$$

$$\underline{} \times \underline{} = \underline{}$$

$$\underline{} \div \underline{} = \underline{}$$

$$\underline{} \div \underline{} = \underline{}$$

4.

$$\underline{} \times \underline{} = \underline{} \qquad \underline{} \div \underline{} = \underline{}$$

$$\underline{} \times \underline{} = \underline{} \qquad \underline{} \div \underline{} = \underline{}$$

Data Analysis

**Family
Note**

In this lesson, your child used multiplication and division to compare data. The **range** of a set of data is the difference between the greatest and the least values. In the table below, the range of the age data is 40 − 8, or 32 years. The **middle value** of a set of data is the number in the middle when the data are arranged in ascending or descending order. In the table below, the middle value of the age data is 12 years.

Please return this Home Link to school tomorrow.

Lily collected information about the ages of people in her family.

Complete.

Name	Age (Years)
Dave	40
Diane	36
Jillian	12
Lara	10
Lily	8

1. The oldest person is _____.

Age: _____ years

2. The youngest person is _____.

Age: _____ years

3. Range of the ages: _____ years

4. Middle value of the ages: _____ years

Fill in the blanks with the name of the correct person.

5. Jillian is about 4 years older than _____.

6. Lara is about 26 years younger than _____.

7. Diane is about 3 times as old as _____.

8. Lara is about $\frac{1}{4}$ as old as _____.

Unit 12: Year-End Reviews and Extensions

Rather than focusing on a single topic, Unit 12 reinforces some of the main topics covered in second grade.

Children will begin the unit by reviewing time measurements—telling time on clocks with hour and minute hands; using alternate names for time; using larger units of time, such as centuries and decades; and keeping track of longer periods of time in years, months, weeks, and days.

Children will also work with computation dealing with multiplication facts and the relationship between multiplication and division.

Finally, children will display and interpret measurement data, with special emphasis on the range, median, and mode of sets of data.

Please keep this Family Letter for reference as your child works through Unit 12.

Vocabulary

Important terms in Unit 12:

timeline A device for showing in sequence when certain events took place. For example, the timeline below shows when the telephone, radio, and television were invented.

factors The numbers being multiplied.

product The result of doing multiplication.

turn-around rule The rule that states that the order of factors does not affect the product.

$$5 \times 6 = 30 \quad 6 \times 5 = 30$$

median The number in the middle when a set of data is organized in sequential order.

range The difference between the greatest and least numbers in a set of data.

mode The value that occurs most often in a set of data.

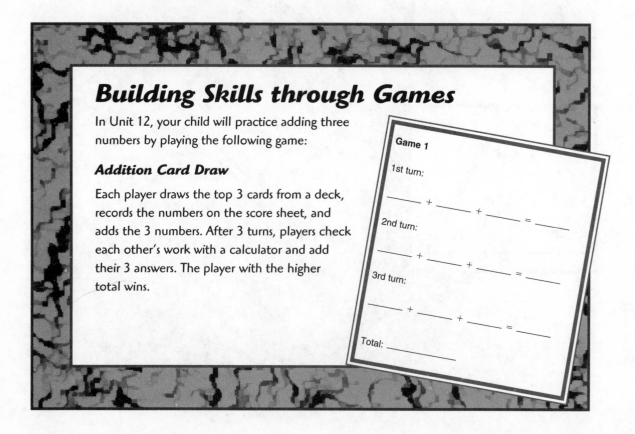

Building Skills through Games

In Unit 12, your child will practice adding three numbers by playing the following game:

Addition Card Draw

Each player draws the top 3 cards from a deck, records the numbers on the score sheet, and adds the 3 numbers. After 3 turns, players check each other's work with a calculator and add their 3 answers. The player with the higher total wins.

Game 1

1st turn:

_____ + _____ + _____ = _____

2nd turn:

_____ + _____ + _____ = _____

3rd turn:

_____ + _____ + _____ = _____

Total:

_____

Use with Lesson 11.10.

Do-Anytime Activities

To work with your child on the concepts taught in this unit and in previous units, try these interesting and rewarding activities:

1. Together, make up multidigit addition and subtraction number stories to solve. Share solution strategies.

2. Make timelines of your lives. In addition to personal historical information, mark various dates of things that interest you, such as musical, sports, historical, and political events.

3. Continue to ask the time. Encourage alternate ways of naming time, such as *twenty to nine* for 8:40 and *half-past two* for 2:30.

4. Continue to review and practice basic facts for all operations, emphasizing the multiplication facts.

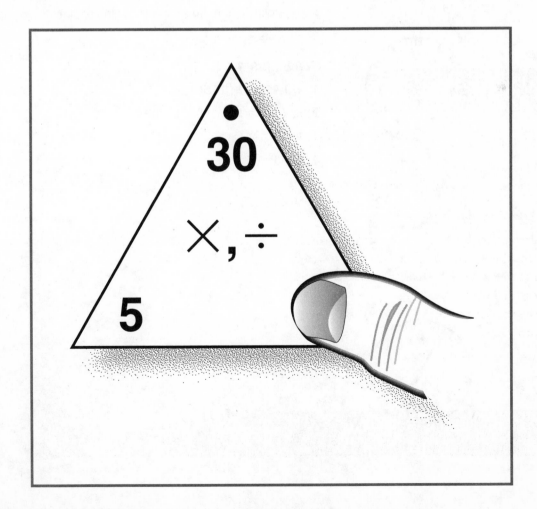

Use with Lesson 11.10.

As You Help Your Child with Homework

As your child brings home assignments, you may want to go over the instructions together, clarifying them as necessary. The answers listed below will guide you through this unit's Home Links.

Home Link 12.1

1. $9 \times 2 = 18$
$2 \times 9 = 18$
$18 \div 2 = 9$
$18 \div 9 = 2$

2. $1 \times 8 = 8$
$8 \times 1 = 8$
$8 \div 1 = 8$
$8 \div 8 = 1$

3. $5 \times 8 = 40$
$8 \times 5 = 40$
$40 \div 8 = 5$
$40 \div 5 = 8$

4. Sample answer:
$4 \times 5 = 20$
$5 \times 4 = 20$
$20 \div 5 = 4$
$20 \div 4 = 5$

Home Link 12.2

1. 4:10   **2.** 8:15   **3.** 10:45

4.

5.

6.

7.

8.

9.

Home Link 12.3

2. 1 hour   **3.** $1\frac{1}{2}$ hours
4. 7 hours   **5.** swimming

Home Link 12.5

1. 7   **2.** 6   **3.** 7   **4.** 3
5. 4   **6.** 4   **7.** 4   **8.** 5
9. 7   **10.** 8   **11.** 7   **12.** 9
13. 6   **14.** 9

Home Link 12.6

1. 30 years   **2.** dolphins and humans
3. 10 years   **4.** ostrich
5. squirrel, cat, lion, horse, ostrich, dolphin, human
6. 30 years

Home Link 12.7

1. a. 1,450   **b.** 1,750
2. a. 2,000   **b.** 1,300   **c.** 700
3. 1,450
4. 1,450

Fact Triangles

Family Note

In class today, your child reviewed the calendar and continued to practice multiplication/division facts. Please spend a few minutes with your child as often as possible practicing facts. You can use Fact Triangles, or you can play a game like *Multiplication Top-It* or *Beat the Calculator*.

Please return this Home Link to school tomorrow.

Fill in the missing number in each Fact Triangle. Then write the fact family for the triangle.

1.

___ × ___ = ___

___ × ___ = ___

___ ÷ ___ = ___

___ ÷ ___ = ___

2.

___ × ___ = ___

___ × ___ = ___

___ ÷ ___ = ___

___ ÷ ___ = ___

3.

___ × ___ = ___

___ × ___ = ___

___ ÷ ___ = ___

___ ÷ ___ = ___

Challenge

4.

___ × ___ = ___   ___ ÷ ___ = ___

___ × ___ = ___   ___ ÷ ___ = ___

Many Names for Times

Family Note

Because clocks with clock faces were used for centuries before the invention of digital clocks, people often name the time by describing the positions of the hour and minute hands. Observe as your child solves the time problems below.

Please return this Home Link to school tomorrow.

What time is it? Write the time shown on the clocks.

1.

_____:_____

2.

_____:_____

3.

_____:_____

Draw the hour hand and the minute hand to show the time.

4.

half-past nine

5.

six fifty

6.

a quarter-to two

7.

quarter-after ten

8.

two thirty

9.

four fifty-five

Family Note

A timeline is a way to display events in sequential order. Timelines may be divided into intervals, such as centuries, years, months, days, and hours. Observe your child as he or she fills in the timeline at the right.

Please return this Home Link to school tomorrow.

Emily's Day at the Beach

1. For each event below, make a dot on the timeline and write the letter for the event above the dot.

A Ate lunch (12:30 P.M.)

B Went fishing in a boat (10:00 A.M.)

C Arrived at the beach (9:00 A.M.)

D Returned from fishing trip (11:30 A.M.)

E Played volleyball (1:30 P.M.)

F Went swimming (2:00 P.M.)

G Drove home (4:00 P.M.)

H Built sandcastles (3:00 P.M.)

2. How long did Emily spend at the beach before she went on the fishing trip? _____ hour(s)

3. How long was the fishing trip? _____ hour(s)

4. How long was Emily's day at the beach? _____ hour(s)

5. Did Emily spend more time playing volleyball or swimming? _____

×, ÷ Fact Triangles

Home Link
12.4

Family Note

Your child has been practicing multiplication facts. Today children reviewed shortcuts for solving multiplication problems with the numbers 2, 5, and 10. Encourage your child to practice with the Fact Triangles over the summer in preparation for third grade.

Cut out the Fact Triangles on these pages. Show someone at home how you can use them to practice multiplication facts.

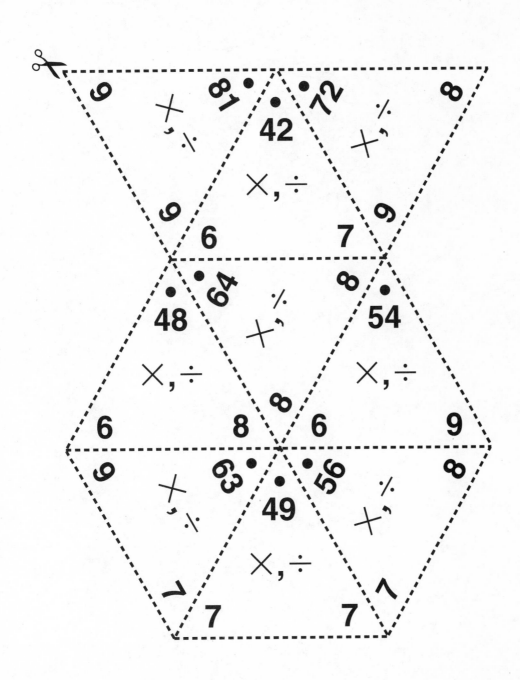

✕, ÷ Facts Practice

Family Note

In this lesson, your child has connected multiplication and division facts by using Fact Triangles and completing fact families. A good way to solve division problems is to think in terms of multiplication. For example, to divide 20 by 5, ask yourself: *5 times what number equals 20?* Since $5 \times 4 = 20$, $20 \div 5 = 4$.

Please return this Home Link to school tomorrow.

Solve these division facts. Think multiplication.
Use the Fact Triangles to help you.

1. $14 \div 2 = $ _____

Think:
$2 \times ? = 14$

14
✕, ÷
2   7

2. $24 \div 4 = $ _____

Think:
$4 \times ? = 24$

24
✕, ÷
4   6

3. $21 \div 3 = $ _____

Think:
$3 \times ? = 21$

21
✕, ÷
3   7

4. $18 \div 6 = $ _____

Think:
$6 \times ? = 18$

18
✕, ÷
6   3

5. $28 \div 7 = $ _____

Think:
$7 \times ? = 28$

28
✕, ÷
7   4

6. $16 \div 4 = $ _____

Think:
$4 \times ? = 16$

16
✕, ÷
4   4

×, ÷ Facts Practice (cont.)

7. 20 ÷ 5 = _____

Think:
5 × ? = 20

20
×,÷
5   4

8. 30 ÷ 6 = _____

Think:
6 × ? = 30

30
×,÷
6   5

9. 35 ÷ 5 = _____

Think:
5 × ? = 35

35
×,÷
5   7

10. 32 ÷ 4 = _____

Think:
4 × ? = 32

32
×,÷
4   8

11. 42 ÷ 6 = _____

Think:
6 × ? = 42

42
×,÷
6   7

12. 63 ÷ 7 = _____

Think:
7 × ? = 63

63
×,÷
7   9

13. 54 ÷ 9 = _____

Think:
9 × ? = 54

54
×,÷
6   9

14. 81 ÷ 9 = _____

Think:
9 × ? = 81

81
×,÷
9   9

Typical Life Spans

Family Note

In this lesson, your child has been reading, drawing, and interpreting bar graphs. Bar graphs are often useful when one wants to make rough comparisons quickly and easily. Provide your child with additional practice in interpreting a bar graph by asking questions like Problems 1–4.

Please return this Home Link to school tomorrow.

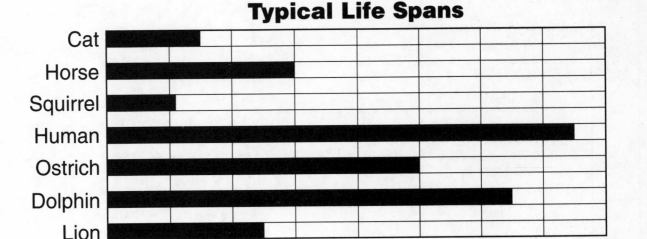

Typical Life Spans

1. About how long do horses live? _____ years

2. Which animals live longer than an ostrich?

   _____

3. About how much longer do lions live than cats? _____ years

4. Which animal lives about twice as long as lions? _____

Typical Life Spans (cont.)

5. List the animals in order from the shortest life span to the longest life span.

Life Spans

shortest:	
longest:	

6. What is the middle value? _____ years
This is the **median.**

Interpret a Bar Graph

Family Note

In class today, your child interpreted graphs and identified the greatest value, the least value, the range, the middle value or the median, and the mode. The mode is the value or category that occurs most often in a set of data. For example, in the bar graph below, the river length of 1,450 miles is the mode.

Please return this Home Link to school tomorrow.

Approximate Lengths of Rivers

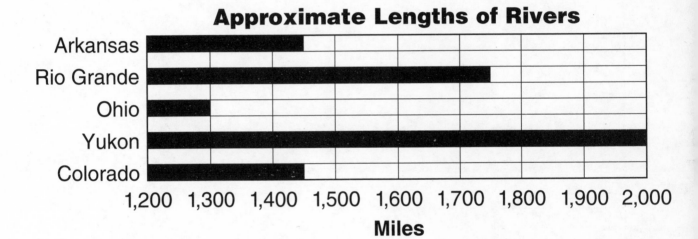

1. **a.** What is the length of the Colorado River? About _____ miles

   b. Of the Rio Grande? About _____ miles

2. **a.** What is the length of the longest river? About _____ miles

   b. What is the length of the shortest river? About _____ miles

   c. What is the difference in length between the longest and the shortest rivers? About _____ miles. This is the **range.**

3. Which river length occurs most often? About _____ miles
   This is the **mode.**

4. What is the middle length of the rivers? About _____ miles
   This is the **median.**

Family Letter

Congratulations!

By completing *Second Grade Everyday Mathematics*, your child has accomplished a great deal. Thank you for all of your support!

This Family Letter is provided as a resource for you to use throughout your child's vacation. It includes an extended list of Do-Anytime Activities, directions for games that can be played at home, an Addition/Subtraction Facts Table, and a sneak preview of what your child will be learning in *Third Grade Everyday Mathematics*. Enjoy your vacation!

Do-Anytime Activities

Mathematics concepts are more meaningful when rooted in real-life situations. To help your child review some of the concepts he or she has learned in second grade, we suggest the following activities for you and your child to do together over vacation. These activities will help your child build on the skills he or she has learned this year and help prepare him or her for *Third Grade Everyday Mathematics*.

1 Fill in blank calendar pages for the vacation months, including special events and dates. Discuss the number of weeks of vacation, days before school starts, and so on.

2 Continue to ask the time. Encourage alternate ways of naming time, such as *twenty to nine* for 8:40 and *a quarter-past five* for 5:15.

3 Continue to review and practice basic facts for all operations, especially those for addition and subtraction.

4 Use Fact Triangle cards to practice basic multiplication and division facts, such as the following:

$2 \times 2 = 4$	$4 \div 2 = 2$
$2 \times 3 = 6$	$6 \div 2 = 3$
$2 \times 4 = 8$	$8 \div 2 = 4$
$2 \times 5 = 10$	$10 \div 2 = 5$
$3 \times 4 = 12$	$12 \div 3 = 4$
$3 \times 3 = 9$	$9 \div 3 = 3$
$4 \times 4 = 16$	$16 \div 4 = 4$
$3 \times 5 = 15$	$15 \div 3 = 5$
$4 \times 5 = 20$	$20 \div 4 = 5$

Building Skills through Games

The following section describes games that can be played at home. The number cards used in some games can be made from 3" by 5" index cards or from a regular playing-card deck.

Addition Top-It

Materials ❑ 4 cards for each of the numbers 0–10 (1 set for each player)

Players 2 or more

Directions

Players combine and shuffle their cards and place them in a deck, facedown. Each player turns up a pair of cards from the deck and says the sum of the numbers. The player with the greater sum takes all of the cards then in play. The player with the most cards at the end of play is the winner. Ties are broken by drawing again—winner takes all.

Variation: *Subtraction Top-It*

Partners pool and shuffle their 0–20 number cards. Each player turns up a pair of cards from the facedown deck and says the difference between them. The player with the greater difference gets all four cards. The player with more cards at the end of play is the winner.

Variation: *Multiplication Top-It*

Players find the product of the numbers instead of the sum or difference. Use the 0–10 number cards.

Pick-a-Coin

Materials ❑ regular die

❑ record sheet (see example)

❑ calculator

Players 2 or 3

Sample Record Sheet						
	Ⓟ	Ⓝ	Ⓓ	Ⓠ	$1	Total
1st turn	2	1	4	5	3	$ 4.72
2nd turn						$ _____
3rd turn						$ _____
4th turn						$ _____
					Total	$ _____

Directions

Players take turns. At each turn, a player rolls a die five times. After each roll, the player records the number that comes up on the die in any one of the empty cells for that turn on his or her own Record Sheet. Then the player finds the total amount and records it in the table.

After four turns, each player uses a calculator to find his or her grand total. The player with the highest grand total wins.

Use with Lesson 12.8.

Multiplication Draw

Materials
- ❑ number cards 1, 2, 3, 4, 5, 10 (4 of each)
- ❑ record sheet (1 for each player)
- ❑ calculator

Players 2–4

Directions

Multiplication Draw Record Sheet
1st draw: _____ × _____ = _____
2nd draw: _____ × _____ = _____
3rd draw: _____ × _____ = _____
4th draw: _____ × _____ = _____
5th draw: _____ × _____ = _____
Sum of products: _____

Shuffle the cards and place the deck facedown on the playing surface. At each turn, players draw two cards from the deck to make up a multiplication problem. They record the problem on a record sheet and write the answer. If the answer is incorrect, it will not be counted. After five turns, players use a calculator to find the total of their correct answers. The player with the highest total wins.

Name That Number

Materials
- ❑ number cards 0–10 (4 of each)
- ❑ number cards 11–20 (1 of each)

Players 2 or 3

Directions

Shuffle the deck of cards and place facedown on the table. Turn the top five cards face up and place them in a row. Turn over the next card. This is the target number for the round.

In turn, players try to name the target number by adding, subtracting, multiplying, or dividing any two of the other faceup cards. Players write their solutions on a sheet of paper. Then they set aside the cards they used to name the target number and replace them with new cards from the top of the deck. Players put the target number on the bottom of the deck and turn over the top card. This is the new target number.

Play continues until there are not enough cards left in the deck to replace the players' cards. The player who has set aside the most cards at the end wins. Sample turns:

Mae's turn: | 4 | 10 | 8 | 12 | 2 | | 6 |

The number to be named is 6. It may be named with $4 + 2$, $8 - 2$, or $10 - 4$.

Mae selects $4 + 2$. She takes the 4, 2, and 6 cards. She replaces the 4 and 2 cards with the top two cards from the facedown deck and then turns over and lays down the next card to replace the 6.

Mike's turn: | 7 | 10 | 8 | 12 | 1 | | 16 |

The number to be named is 16.

Mike can't find two cards to name 16. He turns over the next card from the facedown deck and places it on top of the 16. The next player tries to name the new target number.

Use with Lesson 12.8.

Fact Power

Addition/subtraction fact families can also be practiced by using the Addition/Subtraction Facts Table. This table can be used to keep a record of facts that have been learned as well.

+,−	0	1	2	3	4	5	6	7	8	9
0	0	1	2	3	4	5	6	7	8	9
1	1	2	3	4	5	6	7	8	9	10
2	2	3	4	5	6	7	8	9	10	11
3	3	4	5	6	7	8	9	10	11	12
4	4	5	6	7	8	9	10	11	12	13
5	5	6	7	8	9	10	11	12	13	14
6	6	7	8	9	10	11	12	13	14	15
7	7	8	9	10	11	12	13	14	15	16
8	8	9	10	11	12	13	14	15	16	17
9	9	10	11	12	13	14	15	16	17	18

Looking Ahead:
Third Grade Everyday Mathematics

Next year, your child will ...

· Explore the relationship between multiplication and division

· Extend multiplication and division facts to multiples of 10, 100, and 1,000

· Use parentheses in writing number models

· Record equivalent units of length

· Use number models to find the areas of rectangles

· Explore 2- and 3-dimensional shapes and other geometric concepts

· Read and write numbers through 1,000,000

· Work with fractions and decimals

· Collect data for yearlong sunrise/sunset and high/low temperature projects

· Use map scales to estimate distances

Again, thank you for all of your support this year. Have fun continuing your child's mathematics experiences throughout the vacation!

Use with Lesson 12.8.